THE
BLUE ELEPHANT
Cookbook
ROYAL THAI CUISINE

THE
BLUE ELEPHANT
Cookbook
ROYAL THAI CUISINE

TEXT BY

John Hellon

PHOTOGRAPHS BY

Tony Le Duc

PAVILION

This edition published in Great Britain in 2006 by
PAVILION BOOKS
151 Freston Road, London W10 6TH
An imprint of Anova Books Company Ltd

First published in Great Britain in 1999 by
Pavilion Books Limited

Designed by Isobel Gillan

ISBN 1 86205 303 0

Set in Perpetua
Colour Reproduction by Anglia Graphics Limited, England
Printed in Singapore by Kyodo Printing Co Ltd

10 9 8 7 6 5 4 3 2

This book can be ordered direct from the publisher. Please
contact the Marketing Department, but try your bookshop first.
Internet: http:// www.blueelephant.com/

Vegetarian recipes are marked with the symbol Ⓥ

The 'hotness' of specific recipes are indicated by the
following symbols:

MEDIUM HOT

HOT

VERY HOT

RIGHT: Green Papaya Salad

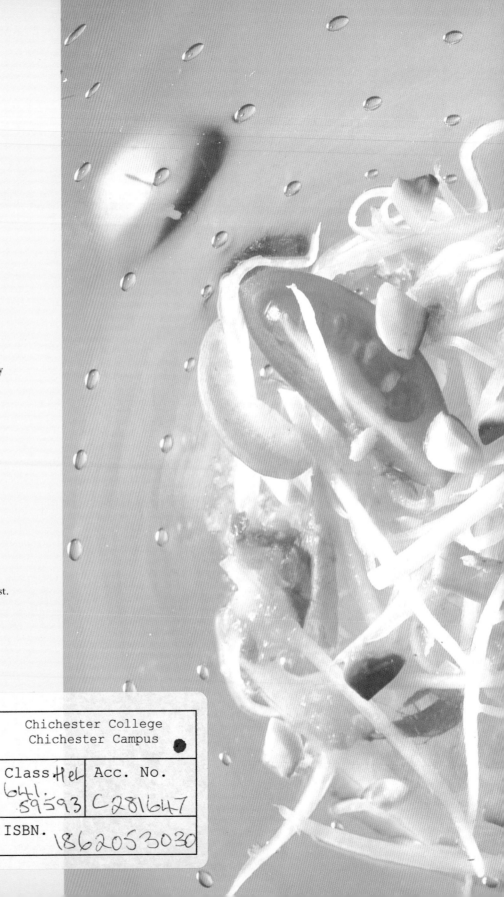

CONTENTS

INTRODUCTION

The people of Thailand like to compare the shape of their country to the head of an elephant, the national emblem. Its trunk is the long narrow isthmus dangling southwards until it terminates at the frontier with Malaysia. Its forehead nudges Burma while Laos and Kampuchea are draped around a fan-shaped ear.

You can also compare the country's outline to the intricate fretwork of a piece in a jigsaw puzzle. This might make a better analogy when it comes to talking about Thai cuisine. For although it is a unique cuisine with its irresistible *leitmotif* of basil, lemongrass, coriander, coconut milk, chillies and a wealth of spices, it is also a synthesis of native traditions and influences from neighbouring countries and further afield. It was the Portuguese, for example, who first brought the now essential chillies from Latin America in the sixteenth century, while the equally ubiquitous rice noodles originated in China.

One of the reasons that Thai cuisine was able so splendidly to absorb and blend these influences is probably cultural. On an intellectual level Buddhism is a great absorber and synthesizer of currents of religious thought. Another reason may well be that Thailand is the only country in Asia never to have been colonized – the very word Thai means free – so there was no reason to resent or resist the contribution of its neighbours.

Of course, cuisine is basically defined by the available produce. Southern Thailand with the Gulf to the east and the Indian Ocean to the west offers above all a superb range of fish and shellfish including squid, prawns, scallops and mussels as well as crabs and lobsters. These are often prepared with milk from the coconuts that grow in profusion on the fringe of the rainforest inland.

The southern region is a melting-pot of culinary influences. The Chinese found similar produce, especially seafood, to that used in their native Canton and prepared it in similar ways: steamed or most often lightly stir-fried with vegetables in a wok. In complete contrast, complex pastes of pounded herbs and spices are the basis of the curries originating in neighbouring muslim Malaysia. Often prepared with meat, especially lamb, their spiciness is attenuated by coconut milk. From Malaysia, too, comes the

Pioneers of The Blue Elephant from left to right: Nooror Somany, Somchai Wayno, Somboon Insusri, and Karl Steppé.

universally popular satay, a kind of miniature kebab of marinated lamb, chicken or fish served with a peanut sauce. In general, the cuisine of the south is the spiciest to be found in the country.

Just as Hinduism represents a current in Thailand's native Buddhism, so Indian cuisine exerts an influence, modified along the way by intervening countries. The north-west of the country, which adjoins Burma, also has its curries. Nowhere in Thailand, however, are curries slowly simmered with a large amount of clarified butter (or indeed any butter) as in India. Instead, they are typically made in the wok with a small amount of vegetable oil and in a surprisingly short space of time.

Both north-west and north-east regions share a preference for glutinous rice. More meat, especially pork, is eaten than in the south, and the city of Chiang Mai is well known for its charcuterie. Recently the cuisine of the north-east, long neglected, has become fashionable. Freshwater fish ranks high among local produce and many dishes are flavoured with lime. Dishes like Green Papaya Salad (see recipe on page 44) and Thai Beef Salad with a Spicy Dressing (see recipe on page 108), illustrate the north east's special predilection for chillies, but the region also features mousse-like preparations of fish or chicken, ground and steamed in pretty banana leaf parcels.

Bangkok, almost needless to say, is a city of dazzling culinary variety. Here the food of the regions vies for attention with the capital's own traditions, based on the produce of the central plains, where the paddy fields produce the best rice, the orchards the best fruit and the gardens a cornucopia of fresh vegetables. It is a supremely gastronomic city, from its myriad street stalls selling rice noodle stir-fries, through popular restaurants – small or vast and garish – to the most distinguished and sophisticated establishments where Royal Thai cuisine is served.

Royal Thai cuisine originated in the king's palace, a city within a city covering an area of a square mile. Young ladies of good family would go into this private world as ladies-in-

Hand-crafted sugar figurines, for decoration in Royal Thai cuisine.

waiting. It acted as a kind of finishing school where the arts of floral decoration, cookery and fruit and vegetable carving were developed to the highest degree. Here each regional dish in the rich spectrum was endowed with more subtlety and refinement, and its presentation enhanced by delicately sculptured mangoes, watermelons, pumpkins, radishes, tomatoes, chillies and root ginger. In this way, cuisine was established as an integral part of the nation's high culture.

Today, the tradition of Royal Thai cuisine is maintained and renewed in the very best restaurants. Like French *haute cuisine*, its roots lie in the rich variety of provincial home cooking. And its standards demand produce of the highest quality prepared with infinite pains to bring out the subtlest of flavours. Inventiveness, too, is common to both traditions, but in the beauty of its presentation, Royal Thai cuisine is unique.

THE STORY OF THE BLUE ELEPHANT

It began as a kind of vision in the mind of an imaginative antiquarian steeped in the arts and crafts of India and South East Asia – and you could say it has remained one.

In the early seventies, Karl Steppé chose Thailand as a convenient base for buying forays into neighbouring countries. Exploring Thailand for the first time, he was overwhelmed by the colours, scents and intricate baroque of the art and architecture that seemed almost to grow organically out of the lush tropical vegetation. He was overwhelmed, too, by the gentle courtesy of the people.

Later, back home in Belgium with his Thai wife, Khun Nooror Somany, whose story is recounted elsewhere in this book, he met two young Thais from the restaurant business, footloose in Brussels. Their names were Khun Somchai Wayno and Khun Somboon Insusri. This accidental conjunction was the catalyst and in 1980 a small Thai restaurant opened its doors. It was called L'Eléphant Bleu, because an elephant is the national emblem of Thailand and blue the national colour.

For Karl Steppé, the restaurant was more or less a hobby, but from the beginning his vision was that it should be a total experience of Thailand, at that time virtually unknown territory for most Europeans, both gastronomically and aesthetically. First and foremost, the vision demanded a totally authentic Thai cuisine, identified by its unique and powerful flavours and artistic presentation. It was prepared by the wives of his Thai associates, Khun Samran Malairman and Khun Laait Pinit, from the highest-quality produce, fresh from Thailand – quite a challenge then, though nowadays the restaurant group flies in some 80 tons of fresh produce every year, selected by Khun Charoen at its Bangkok office.

The dining room was decorated with art and craft objects, selected with an infallible eye from Karl's antique shop and worth twice the investment in the restaurant itself. They were surrounded by exotic flowers and plants. The primary objective, Karl admits, was to give him pleasure rather than to make money. However, the experience the team had created for customers in fulfilment of his vision proved to be

LEFT AND RIGHT: The Blue Elephant restaurants genuinely replicate the beauty and atmosphere of Thailand.

enormously popular. Within a year it was necessary to invest in a brand new kitchen to meet demand. More or less accidentally, the hobby had turned into a business.

In 1982, L'Eléphant Bleu more than doubled in size and an evocative setting was created with the resourceful collaboration of designer Yves Burton, who had previously designed Karl's shop. Customers flocked to sit in comfortable bamboo chairs around tables exquisitely laid with bronze cutlery and china of unique design. The tables nestled in a tropical paradise of trees, plants and flowers which half concealed, half revealed, antique Buddhist statuary, carved architectural details and embroidered textiles. And the customers found themselves cosseted by an endlessly attentive and smiling staff dressed in colourful traditional costumes.

It could have ended there, but as well as vision and an innate talent for management, Karl Steppé and Nooror are gifted with entreprenurial skills. Two more friends and entrepreneurs, Khun Chalngura Jahau and Khun Phouthavong Thaviseuth entered the picture, and in 1985 they launched The Blue Elephant in London, created by the Brussels team joined by chef and new partner Khun Chang and other collaborators.

It was a brave leap in the dark. A dilapidated building on Fulham Broadway, housing an abandoned workshop, was converted at enormous expense into another luxuriant vision of Thailand, much larger than the Brussels original, again designed by Yves Burton, who at this time became a partner in the group. Professional experts were dubious about its chances of success. Fingers were crossed in Brussels and London. Jahau recalls that on the opening day they expected few customers, maybe none at all. Instead the restaurant was full. And, although it has subsequently doubled in size, it has remained full ever since. Restaurant critics were enthusiastic and The Blue Elephant was selected by *The Times* as best oriental restaurant of the year.

Copenhagen followed, the first Blue Elephant to be located in a hotel, the Radisson SAS Scandinavia, where it quickly established itself as one of the city's most distinguished restaurants. And then came another cliffhanger. Even with London under its belt, the challenge of Paris, the world's most demanding restaurant environment, was a daunting one for the group. Much time was spent searching for a promising location. Eventually the right premises were found in the Rue de la Roquette in the Bastille district, just as it was becoming fashionable. Once again, money was lavished on the interior. A Thai village was recreated with carved wooden elements imported from Thailand, a spectacular waterfall splashed gently in the background and, as always, a forest of greenery surrounded the dining tables.

While ready to be charmed by decor, Parisians are too discriminating to accept anything but excellence on their plates. Finally, it was the quality and authenticity of The Blue Elephant's cuisine, with its blend of centuries-old recipes and creative new variations, that guaranteed the restaurant's resounding success.

After a period of consolidation, The Blue Elephant is once again on the move, with new restaurants mainly situated in hotels. They can now be experienced in New Delhi at the Intercontinental, in Dubai at the Al Bustan Rotana and in Beirut at the Searock Hotel. At the time of writing, restaurants are planned for Abu Dhabi, Malta and Lyon, where the Blue Elephant will stand alongside the world-renowned establishments at the epicentre of French gastronomy.

To meet the growing need for expert chefs, the group will open its own school in Bangkok, incorporating a working restaurant. However, The Blue Elephant will never become a chain in the popular sense — it is much too personal and uncompromising an enterprise for that. All the pioneers named in this story and many more remain part of the group and the atmosphere is that of an extended family. Nevertheless, more Blue Elephants are likely to emerge in major cities around the world wherever there are people ready to share Karl Steppé's extraordinarily successful vision.

WINES & ROYAL THAI CUISINE

How to ensure a happy marriage

BY MANUEL DA MOTTA VEIGA

Wine might not be the first drink you think of when planning a Thai meal. And it's true that in Thailand, beer is often the drink of choice, combined with a taste for liquor with food, specifically whisky. Yet, though few foreigners know about it, wine made from fermented grapes has long been produced and consumed in Thailand. Admittedly, though, with the addition of sugar syrup, it is only distantly related to wine as the West knows it. More recently, however, a large vineyard has been established in Loei in the mountainous north-eastern region of the country, where French varieties of vine are grown and French techniques of vinification are used.

Nowadays the world's wines are becoming more and more popular. Wine merchants are springing up everywhere, as are books and magazines devoted to wines. And, surprisingly, more wine is drunk by Thais than by any other Asian people, with the exception of the Japanese.

Over the years at The Blue Elephant, we have put a lot of thought and research into matching wines with the powerful and spicy flavours of Royal Thai cuisine. Overall, we have found that the golden rule is to pick wines that are themselves spicy, or redolent with ripe fruit, even crystallized fruit notes. To temper the spiciness of the food, they are likely to be sweeter than the wines you might choose to complement a European meal; in general, young, fresh, well-made 'petits vins' – little wines – rather than the grander, aged and complex wines of, for example, Bordeaux.

It is outside the scope of this book to list even a fraction of the wines that would meet these criteria. We hope that this brief review will point you in the direction of some (mainly inexpensive) wines that we think fit the bill and provide a useful starting point for your own experiments in the delightful pastime of matching wines to Royal Thai cuisine.

For both red and white wines, three French regions stand out; Alsace, the Loire and the South encompassing the Rhône valley, Provence and Languedoc-Roussillon.

Some wines are specially chosen for The Blue Elephant.

Burgundy, too, should not be forgotten. Further afield, we especially recommend some white wines from New Zealand and South Africa, some reds from the United States and Australia and both reds and whites from Chile and Spain.

White wines

Starting from northern France, among the white wines of Alsace, our choice includes Pinot Blanc, Pinot Auxerrois, Tokay-Pinot and, best of all, the sensationally spicy Gewürztraminer.

In the Loire, Vouvray, Côteaux du Layon and Montlouis are the wines to look for and, more extravagantly, certain great Sancerres. The pronounced character of these wines will complement rather than compete with many Thai dishes.

In the Côtes du Rhone, the choice ranges from the particularly good value for money simple Côtes du Rhone *appellation*, Côtes du Rhone Villages, Laudun, Sablet and similar wines in the south of the region, to the more rarified Hermitages, Crozes Hermitages and Saint-Joseph.

Côteaux du Languedoc is a safe bet among the wines of the Languedoc-Roussillon region. You can also find excellent value for money among some of the country wines of the region, carefully made from fine grape varietes such as Chardonnay and Viognier.

Some superb white wines are to be found across the Pyrenees and westwards at Ribera del Duero in Galicia. Made from local grape varieties, many are exceptionally powerful and fruity, a particularly fine match for Thai spiciness and reminiscent of some of the more exotic wines made outside Europe.

For quality combined with excellent value for money, Chile ranks high. Look for wines from the Maipo valley and nearby Valdevieso made from European grape varieties.

Recently, New Zealand has begun to produce some exceptionally fine exotic whites with the intense fruitiness to complement Thai cuisine. Look out for wines from the Marlborough region and, for a very special treat, Cloudy Bay.

The white wines of Stellenbosch, South Africa, are well known. To go with Thai food, you might also try Constancia from the Cape, a distinguished, sweet Muscat-based wine.

Red wines

Starting this time in the south of France, where the sun gives an especially lively fruitiness to the wines, the Languedoc-Roussillon region provides a wide and mainly inexpensive choice, including Côteaux de Langeudoc, Minervois, Corbières and Côtes du Roussillon Village.

The red wines of Provence have all the sun-ripened character that the name of the region suggests. The well-balanced Bandol is well worth seeking out, as are certain Côtes de Provence or Côtes de Baux de Provence.

Back in the southern part of the Côtes du Rhone region, the simple *appellation* Côtes du Rhône or Côtes du Rhône Village, made predominately from Syrah/Shiraz grapes, are a powerful accompaniment to Thai dishes, as are Châteauneuf-du-Pape, Gigondas, Côteaux de Tricastin and some Côtes du Lubéron. Further north, come the sought-after Crozes-Hermitages, Hermitages, Saint-Joseph and Côte-Rotie.

A little further north still, young Burgundies such as Côtes de Beaune – Chassagne-Montrachet, Savigny, Volnay, Vosne-Romanée, Monthelie – as well as Côtes Chalonaises – Givry, Rully and Mercurey – provide winelovers with some special, if rather extravagant, treats.

You may find that the particular light astringency of red wines in the Loire region provides a pleasing contrast to Thai spiciness. We particularly recommend Chinon, Saumur-Champigny, Bourgueil and Saint-Nicolas de Bourgueil, not forgetting Anjou, source of The Blue Elephant's house red.

In Galicia, Spain, Ribera del Duero produces some exciting reds with the exotic character to match its whites. And, once again, the Maipo Valley of Chile is a reliable source of exceptionally good value for money, well-made red wines.

Northern California comes into its own with superior Cabernet Sauvignon reds, while Oregon produces perhaps lesser known but extremely good-quality Burgundy-type wine from Pinot Noir grapes, very much at home with Thai flavours.

And then, of course, there's Australia and the splendid reds made in Victoria and New South Wales, especially those using Syrah/Shiraz grapes entirely or combined with Cabernet. These wines have the peppery spice of Côtes du Rhone, intensified by the Australian climate, and they provide a similarly powerful accompaniment to a Thai meal.

Rosé wines

Very assertive rosés are a good choice, such as Tavel and Côtes de Provence, Bandol, Côteaux du Languedoc and other rosé wines from Languedoc-Roussillon. And for a real winelover's rosé, certain Bourgogne de Marsannay rosés are well worth seeking out.

Champagne

Our young, fresh, spicy or fruity criteria for wines to accompany Thai cuisine have tended to favour less expensive wines. The right champagne, however, will be rich in Chardonnay grapes and, accordingly, one of the more expensive makes. Best of all, to go with many Thai dishes, is Pink Champagne.

Serving wine

Champagne and rosé wines should, of course, be served chilled. White wines should be only slightly chilled. Some of the young and spicy red wines that we recommend most highly to go with Thai food may also be served slightly chilled (ideally between 12°C and 14°C).

Staff dressed in traditional costumes represent the charm and courtesy of Thailand.

FRUIT & VEGETABLE CARVING

The art and craft of vegetable and fruit carving was developed at the Royal Court of Thailand, where it reached a high level of sophistication.

BY VINAI SOOKMA

Once upon a time it was the custom to carve all the cooked vegetables and fresh fruit which was to be eaten at the table. Nowadays most of the carving has a purely decorative function, though skilled craftsmen can still turn their hand to removing invisible cores or stones from fresh fruit, while leaving it to be served whole and apparently untouched.

Spectacular pieces are fashioned from groups of watermelons and pumpkins. Long papayas are transformed into boats carrying smaller works, while yams are carved into bowls to contain a carved bouquet or to serve curries or rice in.

Vegetable and fruit carving is a skill that takes years to perfect but with patience, practice and a steady hand you can add an elegant finishing touch to your Thai dinner party. Here are four not too difficult examples.

You will need a small, sharp knife with a pointed end and a fine gouge. There are Thai gouges made especially for vegetable and fruit carving. A fine gouge intended for lino or wood cutting from your nearest art supplier will suffice.

Choose vegetables as fresh and as large as possible, and store them in the refrigerator before use.

RADISH FLOWER

1. Cut off the stem end of the radish to make a flat base for it to stand on.
2. Using the gouge, cut out a shallow star in the other end of the radish, giving it up to eight points.
3. Again using the gouge, starting in the interstices between the star points and leaving enough red skin to outline the star shape, cut away narrow petal-shaped wedges, leaving a space of about 1 cm/$\frac{1}{2}$ in above the base so that the wedges remain firmly attached.
4. Repeat point 3. to cut away the remaining wedges of skin, again taking care to leave enough skin at the top to outline the star shape and space at the base to leave the wedges attached.
5. Place the completed radish flower in cold or iced water. After about 15 minutes the 'petals' will open out of their own accord.

CARROT LEAF

Use a very large and regular tube-shaped carrot about 3.5cm/1$\frac{1}{2}$in in diameter.

1. Cut off the root end of the carrot, peel a length of about 6cm/2$\frac{1}{2}$ in of carrot, using a potato peeler if you wish, and cut it off.
2. Cut a tapering wedge from the top to the bottom of the piece of carrot, about $\frac{1}{3}$ of its total volume.

3. Trim the edges from the sides of the tapering end of the wedge, to make a pointed shape.
4. Cut two parallel V-shaped grooves in the centre of the wedge from the top to within 1 cm/$\frac{1}{2}$ in of the pointed tip.
5. Cut a series of small diagonal grooves in a fishbone configuration from each channel towards the edge of the carrot. (Do not cut the centre between the two channels.) With the narrow end of the piece of carrot upwards these wedges should point upwards.
6. Cut out V-shapes from the outer edges of the carrot in between every other diagonal wedge. The result is a leaf with veins and a serrated edge. Set aside in cold or iced water until needed.

CARROT FLOWER

Use a very large and regular tube-shaped carrot about 3.5cm/1$\frac{1}{2}$in in diameter.

1. Cut off the root end of the carrot and peel off about 5cm/2in of skin, using a potato peeler if you wish.
2. Using the gouge, cut shallow grooves lengthways in the peeled part of the carrot as though it were a Grecian column.
3. Cut about 20 very thin slices off the grooved carrot. The slices should have a finely deckled edge.

Exquisite Thai beauty.

4. Peel and cut off a further 5cm/2in of carrot. Carve one end into a slightly rounded shape. The other end should provide a flat base. Cross hatch the rounded end with the gouge to make it look like the centre of a flower.
5. Using the knife and cutting downwards towards the base, make three rows of acute diagonal incisions in the sides of the piece of carrot in a fish scale configuration.

Carrot and white radish combine to form this delicate Thai lily flower.

2. Make eight incisions to a depth of one layer around the onion from the top to about 2 cm/³⁄₄ in from the base. Peel away the layer, being careful to leave the segments attached at the base.

3. Repeat the operation on the second layer, staggering the incisions so that the segments overlap with the segments of the outer layer. Continue to repeat the operation until you reach the centre. Alternatively, after peeling away several layers, hollow out the centre.

4. Trim the segments into the pointed shape of lotus leaves. If you have hollowed out the centre, carve a length of carrot as described in the instructions above to make a flower centre and place it in the centre of the onion.

This method can also be used to make a flower from the base of a leek. But it is a more delicate operation.

Sugar craft is an ancient Thai art spun to perfection at The Blue Elephant.

6. Push the slices into the incisions which will hold them in place like petals around the centre of a flower.

7. Place the completed flower in cold or iced water. After about 15 minutes the 'petals' will curl into an elegant shape.

ONION LOTUS
Use a large Spanish onion.

1. Peel the onion and cut a thin slice off the root end, forming a base and leaving the layers of onion firmly attached. Cut a slice about 1 cm/½ in thick off the top.

GOING TO MARKET

The Thai larder and how to pick and store fresh produce.

BY KHUN CHAROEN TIANGROJRAT

Aubergines (Eggplants)
None of the Thai varieties of aubergine exactly resembles the common Western variety. The standard Thai variety is small, about 2.5cm / 1in in diameter and may be found in Thai grocers. Alternatively, substitute standard aubergine. There is no Western substitute for pea aubergines, however, which resemble small green berries and come in clusters.

Banana leaves
These very large green leaves, from which pieces are cut and made into packages secured with toothpicks for steaming other ingredients, can be obtained fairly easily in Thai and other oriental stores. A less aesthetic substitute is grease-proof paper (baking parchment) tied with string. Banana leaves should be strong, firm and an unblemished green. Make sure they are dry before storing in the refrigerator. They can also be kept in a cool place with good air circulation and out of the sun. In either case use within a week.

Basil
Bai horapa or Thai basil (confusingly sometimes referred to as both holy basil and sweet basil) has a distinctive aniseed / licorice taste, one of the basic flavours that typify Thai cuisine. It is worth seeking it out in Thai grocers. Lemon basil, more occasionally used, is slightly minty. The basil commonly used in the west is a poor substitute for either.

Unless otherwise indicated, Thai basil should be used when basil is listed as an ingredient in recipes.

Look for fresh, unblemished leaves. Stored in the refrigerator in a perforated plastic or paper bag they will keep for five to eight days.

Beancurd – see Tofu
Dry beancurd pastry is available from Thai grocers.

Cardamom
An aromatic pod, widely available at oriental grocers. The white variety is rarer and can be found at Thai grocers.

Chillies (Chilli peppers)

Chillies exist in many varieties. Two – large chillies and bird's eye chillies – are indicated in recipes in this book. 'Large chillies' refer to chillies about 7.5cm/3in long, which can be green, orange or red, or varied in colour. They are of average heat and this can be reduced by removing the seeds. 'Bird's eye chillies' are very small and extremely hot. Always wear rubber gloves when cutting open and working with chillies and *never* rub your eyes!

Chilli sauce

As opposed to the sweet and sour chilli sauces, for which you will find recipes, chilli sauce is a bottled product. The Thai variety can be found in Thai grocers but Tabasco or Tabasco-type sauces may be substituted if necessary.

Chinese mushrooms

These dried mushrooms, also known as black mushrooms, are readily available in oriental food stores. They should be soaked in warm water for at least 15 minutes before use.

Coconut milk and cream

Coconut milk is made by pouring warm water over grated fresh coconut flesh, then straining the liquid through muslin. If left to stand, a thick 'cream' will rise to the surface. We recommend using the readymade canned products rather than the powdered ones – both are readily available.

Coriander (Cilantro)

Fresh coriander is an ingredient in most Thai recipes and an essential, typifying flavour. The roots and stems (about 7.5 to 10cm/3 to 4in of stem attached to the root) are pounded and used in cooking while the leaves are used as a garnish. Roasted coriander seeds and powder do not have the same flavour as fresh coriander and should not be used as a substitute. Fresh coriander is readily available, especially in oriental or hispanic stores, but make sure the roots, as large as possible, are attached and the leaves are fresh and unwilted.

Curry pastes

While we recommend you make your own pastes using the recipes in this book, readymade curry pastes are easily available in Thai and some other oriental food stores.

Fish sauce

Fish sauce, an indispensable flavouring in Thai cuisine and a frequent replacement for salt, is made by packing fish into a barrel and allowing them to ferment. The liquid is then drawn off. Unappealing as this may sound to Western ears, Thai fish sauce is quite mild and has a mellow, un-fishy flavour when cooked.

Galangal

Galangal, also known as Kha, belongs to the ginger family but is harder with a lighter, pinkish flesh. It is available in Asian food stores but, if necessary, common root ginger can be substituted. Pick the whitest available galangal roots with the minimum of eyes.

Garlic

The garlic cloves listed as an ingredient in our recipes refer to cloves of average size taken from a stem with a white, papery outer skin. Green garlic is much milder.

Ginger

Fresh root ginger should always be used. Select firm roots with the minimum of protuberances. Ground ginger has a completely different flavour and is not a substitute.

Jasmine essence

Obtainable at Thai grocers.

Kaffir lime leaves and rind

Kaffir lime leaves, (also known as makrude leaves), are a common ingredient and have a lemony flavour. Cut away the central stem of the leaf, which is too bitter and slice the leaf with scissors. Not always easy to find fresh, kaffir lime leaves can also be bought dried at oriental stores. The fresh leaves should be shiny and unblemished. Stored in a perforated plastic or paper bag they will keep for ten days in the refrigerator or in a cool place with good air circulation. A few recipes call for zest of kaffir lime rind and, if necessary, zest of common lime can be substituted.

Kha
See Galangal

Krachai
Another type of ginger with a slightly stronger flavour and long, thin, finger-like roots. Select pieces with many roots, brown but not too dark in colour.

Lemongrass
Lemongrass is another indispensable flavouring that typifies Thai cuisine. It is readily obtainable in oriental food stores. The coarser, upper part of the stem should be discarded. Select large stems, light green and straight, without bruising or ridges. Lemongrass will keep for seven to ten days in the refrigerator or in a cool place with good air circulation.

Makrude leaves
See Kaffir lime leaves.

Monosodium glutamate
A type of salt which occurs naturally in many foods, crystallized and used as a taste enhancer, especially in the Far East. Because it has been suggested that monosodium glutamate may have disagreeable effects on some people, it is not used in the kitchens of the Blue Elephant.

The Blue Elephant has developed a unique special sauce to enhance the taste of dishes which would otherwise call for monosodium glutamate. The recipe is on page 152. If you would prefer to use a readymade product containing MSG we recommend Maggi Liquid Seasoning in the same quantities indicated in the recipes for Blue Elephant special sauce.

Mungbeans
A yellow bean with a green shell. The beans are used in desserts.

Noodles and vermicelli
Made from rice, Thai noodles are flat like tagliatelli and come in various widths. Also made from rice, vermicelli is fine and round. All are readily available. Bean vermicelli is prepared with flour made from mung beans and can be purchased at Thai grocers.

Onions
Spanish onions are usually specified in our recipes. These are the large round onions with light brown outer skin and white flesh. They have a mild flavour. Red onions should be used when specified. They are sweeter and have a slightly caramelized flavour when cooked.

Oyster sauce
Widely available in bottles, oyster sauce is made from oyster juices, soya and salt. It has a savoury, not a fishy flavour.

Palm sugar
A coarse, golden brown sugar in paste form, traditionally made from the sap of the Palmyra or sugar palm but now from the coconut palm. Brown cane sugar can be substituted if necessary.

Peppercorns
Peppercorns on the branch are available at Thai and Chinese grocers.

Papaya sauce
A commercial product available at Thai grocers.

Potato flour
Potato flour is available at Thai and Chinese grocers. Cornflour may be substituted.

Rice
Readily available, American long-grain rice is a suitable general-purpose rice. Sticky rice, also called glutinous rice, is a starchy white short grain rice available in oriental food stores.

Rice pastry
Rice pastry, also known as spring roll pastry and used for wrapping fillings for deep-frying, is availabe in sheets at Thai and Chinese grocers.

Shrimp paste
An ingredient of Nam Prik Phao sauce (see page 152), this pungent, salty paste is available canned or bottled at oriental food stores. A possible substitute is anchovy paste.

Soy sauce
There are two principal types of soy sauce; light and dark. The light, salty one is most frequently used. The dark one is thickened and sweetened with molasses. Use Chinese rather than Japanese soy sauces for Thai cookery. Unsweetened black soya sauce is obtainable at Thai and Chinese grocers.

Spring roll pastry
See rice pastry.

Sweet dry radishes
Obtainable at Thai and Chinese grocers.

Sweet turnip pickled in honey
Obtainable at Thai and Chinese grocers.

Tamarind juice
Tamarind juice is, in fact, an infusion of tamarind pulp and is available in oriental food stores. A possible substitute is lemon juice in a larger quantity.

Tapioca flour
Obtainable at Thai grocers. Cornflour can be used instead.

Thai parsley
Somewhat similar in appearance to a spring onion (scallion), but without the bulb, the flavour of Thai parsley is similar to a blend of standard parsley and lemongrass. It provides a very typical note in salads and is obtainable at Thai grocers.

Toey leaves
Also known as pandanus leaves, these are long, flat blades, bright green in colour, obtainable at Thai grocers. Reject leaves if the ends are yellowed. Store in the refrigerator in a perforated plastic bag or paper and use within ten days.

Tofu (also referred to as beancurd)
Used as a substitute for meat and fish in vegetarian recipes, tofu is high in protein, low in saturated fats and calories and contains no cholesterol. It is easily obtainable pressed into blocks. The cubed variety is ready deep-fried and can be found in Chinese supermarkets.

Turmeric
Turmeric is a small variety of ginger with an intense orangey-yellow flesh which imparts colour to a dish. It can sometimes be obtained in Asian food stores but the readily available powdered version may be substituted. Reject roots with holes and store in a cool place with good air circulation. Use within two weeks.

Vermicelli
See Noodles.

Yard long beans
These green podded beans are up to 60cm/2ft long. If unobtainable fresh at an oriental food store, French beans may be substituted but, of course, a larger number will be required. Select straight beans with unblackened ends.

Yellow bean paste
Used in the preparation of Blue Elephant Special Sauce (see page 152), yellow bean paste is obtainable at Thai grocers.

COOKING THAI

A meal in Thailand is not divided into separate

courses. All the dishes are brought to the table

at the same time and diners help themselves to

some of each, picking and mixing!

Equipment

Very little extra equipment is needed to cook Thai food in the average Western kitchen, but one essential is a wok, the shape of which facilitates stir-frying. A wok should be heavy with a firm base, so that both hands are left free for stirring/tossing ingredients with a pair of wooden spatulas, cooking them rapidly over a thin film of vegetable oil. Stir-frying, if you've never tried it, is a quickly and easily acquired knack and you are certain to enjoy it!

It is crucial that the oil in the wok reaches and maintains a high temperature – electric hotplates are not ideal for achieving this. Since the wok is by far the most frequently used piece of equipment in Thai cooking, you might consider buying an electric one with its special element-containing base and thermostatic control.

If you have not already got one, a conventional steamer is a virtual necessity. Bamboo steaming trays are an attractive way of serving steamed dishes like Dim Sim (see recipe on page 30), but are not really necessary.

Deep-frying, another everyday Thai cooking method, does not require special equipment, athough we do recommend the use of an electric fryer for safety, convenience and the possibility of controlling the temperature of the oil accurately with a thermostat. Long-handled sieves are necessary for dipping ingredients into deep-frying oil or bouillon. You should also have a large, flat, perforated spoon.

We think a small pestle and mortar is essential. Over and over again our recipes will ask you to pound garlic cloves, coriander roots and stems and/or other ingredients together in a mortar. The reason we specify this method is not only that it is the most traditional and the best, but also because usually the quantities involved are too small to make using a mincer, blender or food processor a practical proposition. By all means use these labour-saving devices when large enough quantities of ingredients are involved to make it worthwhile!

An essential piece of equipment in Thai cooking, is the wok.

A traditional waterside market in Bangkok.

We expect that, as an enthusiastic cook, you will already have sharp kitchen knives, one or more chopping boards, mixing bowls and plenty of wooden spatulas and spoons. One last, inexpensive item you might like to stock up on is a supply of small plastic containers with tight-fitting lids. With the very small quantities of a quite large number of fresh vegetables that many of our recipes call for, you are likely to find yourself with rather a lot of leftover ingredients. These can be kept fresh in the refrigerator in the containers and used for your next Thai meal.

Thai menus

Generally speaking, a meal in Thailand is not divided into separate courses. All the dishes are brought to the table at the same time and diners help themselves to some of each, picking and mixing! Even the soups are part of the main meal. Indeed, the strong flavours and spiciness of many of them are designed for you to punctuate your meal with the occasional spoonful. Assuming you are working single-handed in an average-size domestic kitchen and wish to serve a meal in this way, we suggest that your menu include a cold item such as a salad that can be prepared in advance, a curry that can be set aside and kept hot for a while after cooking and not more than one stir-fry, one deep-fry and one steamed dish. Note that dishes like Salmon Soufflé (see recipe on page 58) and Thai Chicken Soufflé (see recipe on page 84), where the ingredients are wrapped in a pretty banana leaf parcel, can be prepared conveniently in advance and simply steamed at the last moment. Plain rice is, of course, an invariable accompaniment to every Thai meal.

Needless to say, you are entirely free to serve your Thai meal in separate courses as in the West. In fact, our list of recipes begins with items most suitable for serving as hors d'oeuvres or cocktail party titbits. There are four suggested Thai menus on page 154 for immediate convenience in deciding what to cook.

Quantities

When they don't indicate the number of pieces the quantity of ingredients will make, our recipes normally specify one serving. This means one serving shared between four persons when four or more dishes are served at the same time, composing a complete Thai meal. Standing alone, the quantities indicated will make one generous individual portion.

The quantities indicated for seasonings are a guide. Trial and error will soon enable you to determine the quantities that suit your individual taste.

Vegetarian dishes

This book contains an unusually wide range of tempting vegetarian dishes. As well as the ones listed separately, recipes that can be easily adapted for preparation without animal or animal-based ingredients are indicated in the list of recipes.

Cooking temperatures

We have indicated deep-frying oil temperatures in the hope that you will be using an electric deep fryer with a thermostat. If you're not, and for oil in the wok, many cookbooks tell you to look for an elusive 'blue haze' rising from the oil that indicates it has reached the right frying temperature. An easier and more reliable method, in our experience, is to take a little piece of what you are about to fry and pop it into the oil. If it sizzles immediately, your oil has reached the right temperature!

For boiling and steaming, our cooking times assume your kitchen is located at or near sea level. If you live at a high altitude (anything over about 1000 metres) you will already be aware that the temperature of water at boiling point reduces as altitude increases, and adjust boiling and steaming times accordingly.

Pounding, chopping and slicing

We've already talked about the advantages of using a pestle and mortar and the need for sharp knives. When our recipes refer to 'coriander roots and stems', we mean the whole root (carefully cleaned) plus about 7cm/3in green stem. The leaves are retained for use as a universal garnish.

Unless otherwise indicated, vegetables should always be sliced diagonally to expose the maximum area to rapid cooking in the wok.

Do make sure that *all* your ingredients are pounded, chopped, sliced or otherwise pre-prepared as indicated in the opening paragraphs of the recipes before you begin to cook. Thai cooking methods are rapid and simple. The pounding, chopping and slicing is more than half the battle!

Floating markets and fragrant Thai soups.

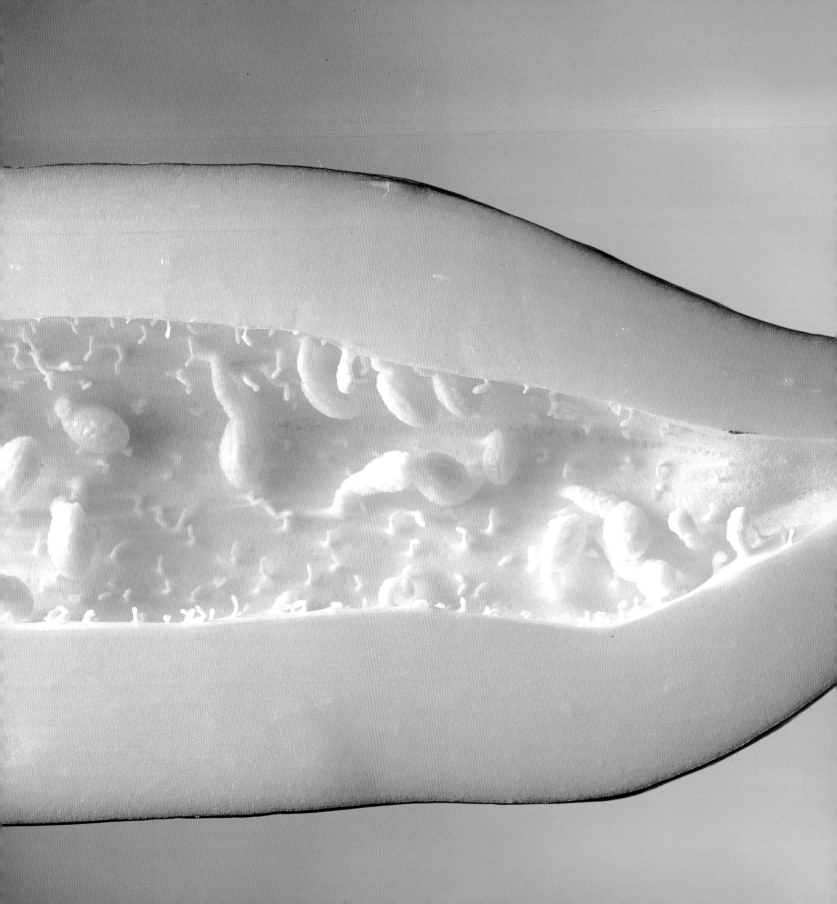

STARTERS

THAI FISH CAKES

Tod Man Pla

Spices and red curry give a hot kick to this popular dish, which is quick and easy to prepare.

makes 1 serving
(8 fish cakes)

200g/7oz fillet of cod or other white fish
200g/7oz squid
2½tbsp Red Curry Paste
  (see recipe on page 151)
1tbsp fish sauce
2tsp sugar
2 kaffir lime leaves, finely chopped
60g/2oz yard-long beans or French beans, cut
  into very thin slices less than 2mm/¹⁄₁₀in thick

½ egg, beaten
vegetable oil for deep-frying
½ tsp crushed, roasted peanuts
Cucumber Sauce to serve
  (see recipe on page 146)

FOR THE GARNISH
mixed green salad leaves

Grind or process the fish and the squid into a smooth paste.

Mix the curry paste, fish sauce and sugar into the fish and squid mixture. Add the kaffir lime leaves and yard-long beans. Fold in the beaten half egg.

Form 8 balls, using about 50g/2oz mixture for each one. Flatten them into discs about 5mm/¼in thick and 6cm/2½in in diameter.

Deep-fry in vegetable oil heated to 180°C/350°F for 3 minutes.

Remove the fishcakes from the oil, drain them on kitchen paper, place on a serving dish on a bed of salad leaves, then sprinkle with the peanuts.

Serve Cucumber Sauce separately in a bowl.

BARBECUED CHICKEN

Kai Sieb Mai

A typically Thai marinade gives the familiar kebab an intriguing twist.

makes 1 serving
(4 pieces)

FOR THE MARINADE
2 cloves garlic, peeled
2 coriander roots and stems
3 branches fresh coriander, finely chopped
½tsp ground white pepper
1tsp whisky
1tsp sesame seed oil
3tbsp unsweetened evaporated milk
2tsp sugar
2tsp Blue Elephant Special Sauce
  (see recipe on page 152)
2tsp vegetable oil
½tsp salt
2tsp papaya sauce (yentafo)
1tsp chilli sauce (Shiracha)

150g/5oz chicken thighs, deboned but with
  skin intact, cut into 8 cubes, each about
  2.5cm/1in wide
30g/1oz mixed red and green bell peppers,
  deseeded
15g/½oz Spanish onion
15g/½oz pineapple wedges
4 cherry tomatoes
4 bamboo skewers 20cm/8in long
Pineapple Sauce to serve
  (see recipe on page 148)

FOR THE GARNISH
mixed green salad leaves
coriander leaves for sprinkling

To make the marinade, pound the garlic, coriander roots and stem together in a mortar until they form a paste, then thoroughly stir all the marinade ingredients together in a bowl.

Marinate the chicken meat for 2 hours. Meanwhile, cut the red and green peppers and the onion into squares about 2cm/¾in wide. (You will need four squares of each of these vegetables.)

On each bamboo skewer, spear first a piece of green bell pepper, then a piece of chicken, onion, pineapple, chicken, red bell pepper, chicken and finally a cherry tomato.

Grill for about 15 minutes until cooked, turning regularly. Arrange on a bed of salad leaves and sprinkle with coriander leaves to serve.

Serve Pineapple Sauce separately in a bowl.

Blue Elephant Spring Roll

Po-Pia Thot

Although this recipe may seem elaborate, it is well worth making as the contrast between the crisp deep-fried rice flour envelope and the texture of the lightly stir-fried contents is quite irresistible!

makes 2 servings (12 pieces)

60g/2oz vermicelli
1½tbsp vegetable oil
1 coriander root and stem, finely chopped
2 cloves garlic, peeled and finely chopped
60g/2oz/⅕ cup raw minced chicken
½ Spanish onion, peeled and finely chopped
40g/1½oz carrot, peeled and cut into julienne strips (matchsticks)
60g/2oz cabbage, finely sliced
30g/1oz celery, finely sliced
60g/2oz leek, finely sliced
2tsp fish sauce

1tbsp Blue Elephant Special Sauce (see recipe on page 152)
1tsp sugar
½tsp ground white pepper
12 sheets rice pastry squares, each 20cm/8in wide
1 egg yolk
Red Sweet & Sour Sauce to serve (see recipe on page 146)

FOR THE GARNISH
mixed green salad leaves

Soak the vermicelli in cold water for 15 minutes and cut into 8cm/3in long pieces.

Heat the oil in a wok until very hot. Add the coriander root and garlic and stir-fry for a few moments.

Add the chicken and, after about 2 minutes, when it is half cooked, add the drained vermicelli. Stir-fry for 30 seconds, then add the remaining vegetables, sauces, sugar and pepper. Continue to stir-fry for about 2 minutes until the vegetables are lightly cooked (al dente). Transfer the mixture to a bowl and allow to cool.

For each spring roll, take about 2tbsp mixture and place it on the pastry. Fold the pastry sheets, roll firmly and seal with egg yolk.

Make a bed of green salad leaves on a serving dish. Deep-fry the spring rolls in oil heated to 180°C/350°F for 3 minutes, drain on absorbent paper and place on the salad leaves. Serve hot with Red Sweet & Sour Sauce in a separate bowl.

For a vegetarian version of this recipe, see page 120.

DIM SIM

Khanom Jeeb

Like the Chinese dim sum, the Thai version is full of flavour and makes an interesting appetizer.

makes 2 servings
(10 pieces)

FOR THE FILLING
200g/7oz white chicken or pork meat, skinned and minced or processed fairly coarsely
60g/2oz/¼ cup peeled prawns, minced or processed fairly coarsely
40g/1½oz/¼ cup finely cubed water chestnuts (available canned)
1 spring onion (scallion), finely chopped
1tsp potato flour
pinch ground white pepper
1tbsp Blue Elephant Special Sauce (see recipe on page 152)

1tsp sugar
pinch of salt
1tbsp vegetable oil

10 pieces wonton pastry
2tsp cooked crabmeat
Dark Soya Sauce for Dim Sum to serve (see recipe on page 149)

FOR THE GARNISH
green salad leaves
fresh coriander leaves for sprinkling

Mix all the filling ingredients together.

Trim the four corners from the pastry. Take one sheet and place it in the hollow of the thumb and forefinger, forming a declivity. Place about 1½tbsp filling in the declivity and press together the top of the sheet to form an open pouch. Continue in this way until you have made 10 Dim Sim.

Dip the base of each one in oil and place in the top half of a steamer. If you are using 2 bamboo baskets instead, place 5 pieces in each one. Put a little crabmeat on top of the filling in each Dim Sim.

Place the baskets on top of each other, placing a lid on the top basket. Steam for 10 to 12 minutes over boiling water.

Arrange salad leaves on individual plates and place 2 pieces on each one. Sprinkle with the fresh coriander leaves.

Serve Dark Soya Sauce separately in small bowls.

PAPER PRAWNS

Koong Hom Pha

Elaborate to prepare, but a great delicacy: three layers of taste and texture to bite into, culminating in the sweet stuffing.

makes 4 servings
(16 pieces)

FOR THE STUFFING
1 clove garlic, peeled
1 coriander root and stem
1 tbsp vegetable oil
50g/1¾oz raw white chicken meat, skinned and minced or processed finely
3 tbsp sugar
1 tsp salt
60g/2oz sweet dry radish, minced or processed
15g/½oz roasted peanuts, crushed

16 medium-sized prawns, shelled and deveined with tails left on
8 spring roll pastry (rice pastry) squares, 21cm/8in wide, halved diagonally
1 egg yolk
vegetable oil for deep-frying
Green Chilli Sweet & Sour Sauce to serve (see recipe on page 146)

FOR THE GARNISH
green salad leaves

To make the stuffing, pound the garlic into a paste with the coriander root and stem in a mortar.

Heat the oil in a wok until very hot, then add the garlic and coriander paste. Stir-fry for 5 seconds then add the chicken and stir-fry for about 3 minutes until cooked on the outside. Add the sugar, stir until it caramelizes, then add the salt. Stir and add the radish and the peanuts. Cook the mixture on a low heat for about 5 minutes until it has thickened. Set aside.

Make a deep slit lengthways in each prawn and fill with the stuffing. Fold the spring roll pastry and roll firmly so that there are no gaps for the oil to seep through. Seal with the egg yolk.

Deep-fry the stuffed and wrapped prawns in oil heated to 180°C/350°F for about 5 minutes, until golden-brown.

Remove the prawns from the oil, drain on absorbent paper and arrange on a serving dish lined with green salad leaves.

Serve Green Chilli Sweet & Sour Sauce separately in individual bowls.

SQUID & PRAWN RISSOLES

Tod Man Khao Phode

The humble rissole is elevated into an intriguing and delicious surprise.

makes 8 pieces

1 clove garlic, peeled
1 fresh coriander root and stem
200g/7oz squid
140g/4½oz prawn meat
pinch ground white pepper
1tsp potato flour
2tbsp Blue Elephant Special Sauce
  (see recipe on page 152)
½tsp sugar
pinch salt

1 egg white
100g/3½oz sweetcorn kernels
50g/2oz white breadcrumbs
vegetable oil for deep-frying
Pineapple Sauce to serve
  (see recipe on page 148)

FOR THE GARNISH
green salad leaves

In a mortar, pound the garlic and coriander root and stem into a paste.

Mince or process the squid and prawn meat together until they are a homogenous paste.

Add the pepper, potato flour, coriander and garlic paste, Blue Elephant Special Sauce, sugar and salt. Stir well in a circular motion. Beat the egg white lightly and fold in. Mix in the corn kernels.

Take about 50g/2oz mixture, roll it in the breadcrumbs and press flat in the form of a disc. Continue until you have made 8 rissoles and deep-fry at 180°C/350°F for about 3 to 4 minutes until golden brown.

Remove the rissoles from the oil, drain on absorbent paper and place on a serving dish lined with salad leaves.

Serve Pineapple Sauce separately in a bowl.

CHICKEN, PORK OR LAMB SATAYS

Satay Kai, Satay Mou and Satay Kae

Originally from the south of Thailand, satays are a universally popular snack food. They make tasty titbits to serve with drinks, as a starter or as an item in a complete Thai meal. If necessary, they can be kept hot for a while before serving.

makes 8 satays
(2 per person)

325g/11oz white chicken meat, skinned, or the
    same quantity of lean pork or lamb, cut into
    16 thin strips, each about 2.5mm/$\frac{1}{10}$in thick
    and 5cm/2in long
8 bamboo skewers

FOR THE MARINADE
2 cloves garlic, peeled
1 coriander root and stem
$\frac{1}{2}$ stem lemongrass
2 toey leaves, chopped
1tsp curry powder
2tsp ground turmeric

1tsp sugar
$\frac{1}{2}$tsp salt
250ml/$\frac{1}{2}$pint/1 cup coconut milk
2tsp Blue Elephant Special Sauce
    (see recipe on page 152)
1tbsp vegetable oil
$\frac{1}{2}$tsp ground white pepper
Peanut Sauce and Cucumber Sauce
    (see recipes on pages 150 and 146) to serve

FOR THE GARNISH
mixed green salad leaves
fresh coriander leaves for sprinkling

To make the marinade, pound the garlic into a paste together with the coriander root and lemongrass in a mortar. Thoroughly stir the paste and all the other marinade ingredients in a bowl.

Add the strips of meat and turn them to ensure they are well coated. Cover and marinate for 2 hours in the refrigerator.

Remove the meat from the marinade and thread two strips in a zigzag on to each bamboo skewer. Grill the satays for about 5 to 6 minutes on each side, turning them and basting with the marinade until cooked through.

To serve, place the satays on the salad leaves in a dish and sprinkle with coriander.

Serve with Peanut Sauce and Cucumber Sauce separately in bowls for dipping.

OPPOSITE FROM LEFT TO RIGHT: Chicken, Seafood and Lamb Satays. *BELOW:* Pork Satay

SEAFOOD SATAY

Satay Talay

Try this seafood variant of the traditional meat satay. It's easily made and pleasantly light (for photograph, see page 34).

makes 2 servings
(8 pieces)

FOR THE MARINADE
1 clove garlic, finely chopped
2tbsp vegetable oil
2tbsp oyster sauce
1½tsp Blue Elephant Special Sauce
    (see recipe on page 152)
pinch of ground white pepper
2tsp sugar

250g/9oz squid, cut into 16 strips, each about
    2.5cm/1in wide by 12cm/5in long

120g/4oz scallops
8 medium-sized prawns weighing about
    80g/3oz in total, shelled and deveined with
    tails left on
8 bamboo skewers
Chilli Sauce to serve (see recipe on page 146)

FOR THE GARNISH
green salad leaves
fresh coriander leaves for sprinkling

For the marinade. Fry the garlic in 2tbsp vegetable oil for about 1 minute until golden brown. Allow the oil to cool.

Mix all the marinade ingredients together, including the oil with the fried garlic. Add the squid strips, scallops and prawns and stir in the marinade until well coated. Cover and marinate in the refrigerator for 2 hours.

Remove the seafood from the marinade and skewer first a rolled-up strip of squid, then scallops, another rolled-up strip of squid and, finally, a prawn rolled up head to tail. Repeat until you have assembled all 8 satays.

Grill the satays for 8 minutes, turning occasionally, until cooked through.

Place the satays on a bed of green salad leaves and sprinkle with the fresh coriander leaves. Serve Chilli Sauce separately in a bowl.

BAGS OF GOLD
Thung Thong

Like spring rolls, Bags of Gold give a lovely contrast of texture between the crisp 'bag' and the soft filling. However, they are easier to assemble, involve only one cooking process and have great visual appeal.

makes 1 serving
(8 pieces)

8 pieces dry beancurd pastry or spring roll pastry, each 12cm/5in square
8 spring onion (scallion) leaves, each about 18cm/7in long
vegetable oil for deep-frying

FOR THE FILLING
1 clove garlic, peeled
2 coriander roots and stems
2 Chinese dried mushrooms
1 spring onion (scallion), finely sliced
160g/5½oz raw minced white chicken meat

30g/1oz cooked crab meat
½tsp ground white pepper
1½tsp Blue Elephant Special Sauce
  (see recipe on page 152)
1tsp sugar
pinch of salt
1 egg
Chilli Sauce to serve
  (see recipe on page 146)

FOR THE GARNISH
green salad leaves

To make the filling, pound the garlic into a paste in a mortar with the coriander roots and stems. Soak the mushrooms for 10 minutes in cold water and slice finely.

Mix all the filling ingredients in a bowl and knead well.

Moisten the beancurd pastry in cold water. Place some of the filling in the centre of each piece and continue until you have made 8 bags.

Soften the spring onion leaves by putting them briefly into hot water. Form pouches by bringing the four corners of the pastry squares together above the filling and tying them together with the spring onion leaves.

Deep-fry for 4 to 5 minutes in oil heated to 180°C/350°F, remove and drain on absorbent paper.

Place the bags on a serving dish lined with green salad leaves and serve hot with Chilli Sauce separately in a bowl.

BANANA FLOWER SALAD

Yam Hua Pee

This unusual and delicious salad is an old traditional Thai recipe. Banana flowers are not always available but watch out for them at your nearest Thai grocers.

makes 1 serving

1 large banana flower
1 tbsp lemon juice
30g/1oz white chicken flesh, grilled and
   shredded
30g/1oz cooked and shelled prawns, coarsely
   chopped
½tbsp dried shrimps, finely crushed
6tbsp Tamarind Sauce (see recipe on page 148)
1tbsp fish sauce
2tsp Nam Prik Phao (see recipe on page 152)

2tsp roasted desiccated coconut
1tbsp coconut milk
3tsp roasted peanuts
coconut shell for serving (optional)

FOR THE GARNISH
shallots, finely sliced
vegetable oil for deep-frying
green salad leaves

To make the golden-fried shallot garnish, deep-fry the shallots in oil for about 2 minutes until golden-brown. Remove and drain on absorbent paper. Set aside.

Cut the banana flower in four vertically. Remove the small, unripe bananas inside and discard, then slice the flowers horizontally into fine segments about 2mm/$\frac{1}{10}$in wide. Add the lemon juice to water, then immerse them for 1 minute so that they remain white.

Mix together all the ingredients, except for the coconut milk and peanuts, in a bowl. Add the coconut milk and peanuts and toss lightly.

Fill a bowl or coconut shell with the salad and place on a bed of green salad leaves. Serve at room temperature, sprinkled with the golden-fried shallots.

VERMICELLI SALAD

Yam Woon Sen

Red chillies give a touch of heat to this unusual salad with its mixture of raw and freshly cooked ingredients.

makes 1 serving

100g/3½oz bean vermicelli
60g/2oz chicken breast, without skin
1 red chilli
2 cloves garlic, peeled
2tsp sugar (reduce amount if scaling up this recipe)
2tbsp lemon juice
2tbsp fish sauce
1tbsp vegetable oil
1 large uncooked prawn, cut into small pieces

1 stick celery, taken from the heart, with leaf, finely chopped
¼ red onion, finely chopped
2 spring onions (scallion), finely chopped
1 small or ½ large (¼ cup) carrot, shredded

FOR THE GARNISH
green salad leaves
coriander leaves for sprinkling

Cover the vermicelli with cold water and soak for 15 minutes. Drain well and cut into 10cm/4in lengths. Mince the chicken breast in a mincer using the fine ring, or processor, taking care not to over-process.

To make the dressing, coarsely grind or process the chilli with one of the garlic cloves and mix with the sugar, lemon juice and fish sauce.

Crush in a mortar the remaining garlic clove. Heat the oil and brown it for a few seconds. Boil the vermicelli for 2 minutes, then drain well. Place the minced chicken and the prawn in a sieve, immerse in boiling water for about 2 minutes until cooked, then drain well.

Place the vermicelli, cooked chicken and prawns in a bowl and add the oil with the browned garlic. Add the remaining ingredients and the dressing and turn the salad gently so that it is well mixed.

Place the salad on a serving dish surrounded by green salad leaves. Sprinkle with coriander.

For a vegetarian version of this recipe, see page 121.

Jungle Salad

Yam Tha Vai

A tempting combination of lightly steamed vegetables, chicken and tuna is given a spicy kick by a powerful curry-flavoured sauce. You may, of course, serve this salad in bowls instead of banana leaf cups, if you wish.

makes 4 banana leaf cups

1 banana leaf
1 slice aubergine (eggplant), about 4cm/1½in wide, 1 peeled carrot and 30g/1oz morning glory, all cut into julienne strips (matchsticks) about 4cm/1½in long
5 pieces baby corn, quartered
60g/2oz yard-long beans or French beans, sliced into 4cm/1½in pieces
30g/1oz/⅓ cup beansprouts
40g/1½oz white chicken flesh, boiled, skinned and shredded

FOR THE SAUCE
2tbsp vegetable oil
2tbsp Red Curry Paste
  (see recipe on page 151)
2tbsp fish sauce
5tbsp coconut milk
3tbsp palm sugar
3tbsp tamarind juice
80g/3oz/⅓ cup tuna fish in brine

FOR THE GARNISH
vegetable oil, for deep-frying
shallots, finely sliced
green salad leaves
sesame seeds for sprinkling

Slice and deep-fry the shallots for the garnish in oil heated to 180°C/350°F until golden brown. Drain on absorbent paper and set aside. Make cups from the banana leaf or use small soup bowls instead.

To prepare the sauce, heat the oil in a wok until very hot. Add the Red Curry Paste and stir-fry for 5 seconds. Add the fish sauce, stir and add the coconut milk, palm sugar and tamarind juice. Mix well, add the tuna fish, remove from the heat and set aside to cool.

Blanch the vegetables, with the exception of the beansprouts, for 3 minutes in boiling water. Add the beansprouts, then quickly remove all the vegetables and plunge them into cold water.

Drain the vegetables and place them in the banana leaf cups. Pour over the sauce and top with the shredded chicken.

Arrange the green salad leaves on a serving dish, place the cups on top and sprinkle them with the sesame seeds and golden-fried shallots.

SUNBURST POMELO SALAD

Yam Som O

This refreshing marriage of citrus fruit, chicken, prawns and typically Thai seasonings makes a splendid starter. It can be prepared a short time in advance and set aside, but preferably not in the refrigerator.

makes 1 serving

20g/¾oz desiccated coconut
2 pomelos
200g/7oz cooked prawns
120g/4oz cooked white chicken meat, skinned
20g/¾oz ground dried shrimps
20g/¾oz roasted peanuts
2½tbsp Nam Prik Phao
  (see recipe on page 152)
3tbsp Tamarind Sauce (see recipe on page 148)

3tbsp fresh lemon juice
3tbsp fish sauce

FOR THE GARNISH
green salad leaves
sliced and golden-fried shallots for sprinkling
20g/¾oz deep-fried dried red chilli
40g/1½oz quail's eggs, hard-boiled and fried

Prepare the garnishes.

Sauté the desiccated coconut in a non-stick frying pan without any oil until light brown.

Slice the pomelos in two with zigzag cuts, using the point of a sharp knife. Scoop out the flesh and set aside, reserving the scooped-out skins.

Mix the remaining ingredients together in a bowl, then add the pomelo flesh and mix in lightly. Place the mixture in the scooped-out half pomelos.

Add the garnishes on top of the half pomelos, arrange the salad leaves on a serving dish and place the pomelos on top. Serve at room temperature.

Green Papaya Salad

Som Tam

A traditional raw salad with a mildly spicy seasoning. Unripe papaya is firm-fleshed so make sure you slice it thinly. (For photograph see detail on page 25.)

makes 1 serving

1 clove garlic, peeled
4 green bird's-eye chillies
30g/1oz yard-long beans or French beans, cut
  into 2cm/¾in pieces
20g/¾oz/⅙ cup dried shrimps
2tbsp palm sugar
3tbsp fish sauce
3tbsp lemon juice

60g/2oz cherry tomatoes, quartered
30g/1oz/⅛ cup roasted peanuts
200g/7oz unripe green papaya, peeled and
  grated into long, thin strips

FOR THE GARNISH
green salad leaves

In a mortar, roughly pound the garlic and chillies. Add the beans and pound, then the shrimps and pound again until crushed.

Add the sugar, fish sauce and lemon juice and stir together. Add the tomatoes and press with the pestle.

Add the peanuts and the papaya and stir until well mixed in.

Serve cold in a round dish lined with the salad leaves.

Seashell

makes 1 serving
(4 pieces)

20g/¾oz butter
2 coriander roots and stems, crushed
3 cloves garlic, peeled and finely chopped
½tsp ground white pepper
1tbsp Blue Elephant Special Sauce (see recipe
  on page 152)
2tsp oyster sauce
150g/5oz scallops (from 1 to 7 per person,
  depending on size)

4 scallop shells or shallow, heatproof bowls
Chilli Sauce to serve (see recipe on page 146)

FOR THE GARNISH
green salad leaves
coriander leaves for sprinkling
4 lemon wedges

Melt the butter in a saucepan and stir-fry the coriander roots and stems and garlic for 1 minute.

Add the pepper, Blue Elephant Special Sauce, oyster sauce and 2tbsp water. Simmer for 2 minutes.

Place the raw scallops on the shells or in the bowls and pour the sauce over them. Grill at the closest position to maximum heat for about 3 minutes until slightly brown.

Place the scallop shells or bowls on a serving dish lined with salad leaves. Sprinkle with coriander and place a lemon wedge on each plate. Serve Chilli Sauce separately in a bowl.

FISHING BASKET

makes 1 serving

FOR THE SESAME SEED SQUID BALLS
2 cloves garlic, peeled
75g/2½oz squid
½tsp ground white pepper
1tsp light soya sauce
2tsp white sesame seeds

FOR THE BATTER
160g/5½oz self-raising flour

4 large prawns, shelled and deveined with tails left on
4 large shelled mussels
4 squid rings
2tbsp white breadcrumbs
vegetable oil for deep-frying
Chilli Sauce to serve
  (see recipe on page 146)

FOR THE GARNISH
green salad leaves

In a mortar, pound the garlic to a paste, then the squid. Or process both successively in a food processor.

Mix together all the ingredients for the squid ball except the sesame seeds. Make 4 balls with the mixture and roll them in the sesame seeds. Set aside.

Make the batter by mixing the flour with 250ml/8fl oz/1 cup water. Dip the prawns, mussels and squid rings in the batter, then roll them in the breadcrumbs.

Heat the oil to 180°C/350°F and deep-fry the squid balls for 1 minute. Add the prawns, mussels and squid rings and fry for a further 3 minutes. Remove and drain on absorbent paper.

Place the seafood on a serving dish lined with the green salad leaves and serve hot with Chilli Sauce separately in a bowl.

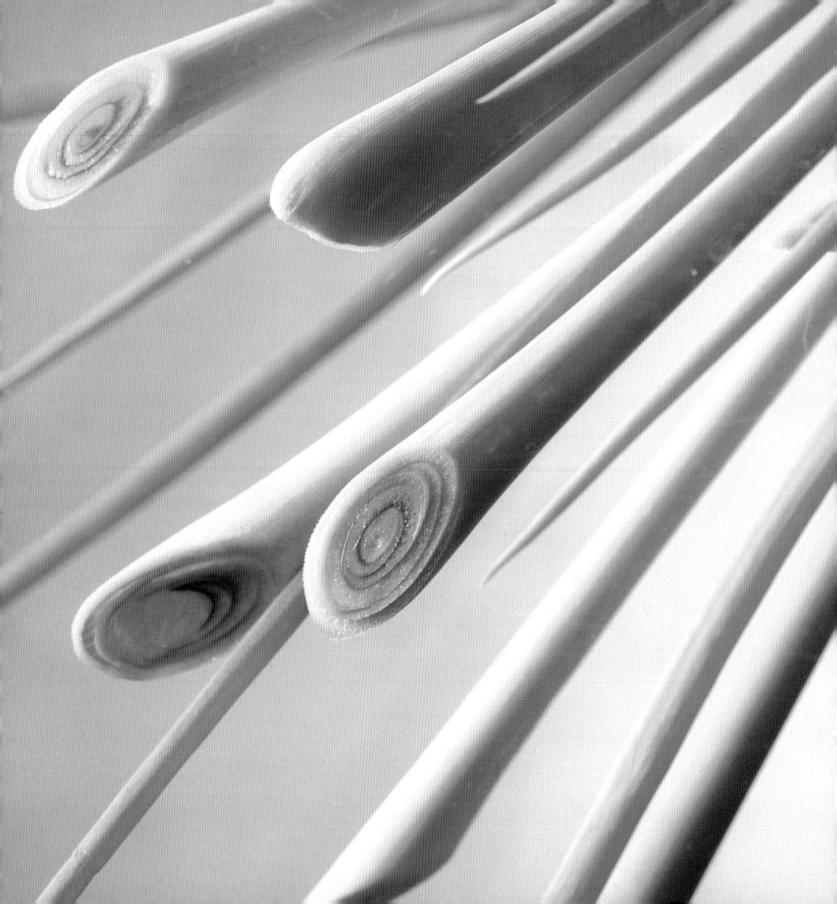

SOUPS

BANGKOK SOUP

Koawteaw Nua

A delicate yet quite substantial soup that is easy and quick to prepare.

makes 4 bowls

75g/2½oz rice noodles
2 cloves garlic, peeled
1½tbsp vegetable oil
700ml/1¼ pints/3 cups beef stock
2 or 3 coriander roots and stems
1 star anise
½tsp ground pepper
2tbsp fish sauce

3tbsp light soya sauce
1½tsp sugar
75g/2½oz/1 cup beansprouts
200g/7oz beef fillet, cut into slices about
    ½cm/⅕in thick
a small handful/¼ cup fresh coriander leaves,
    finely chopped
1 spring onion (scallion), finely chopped

Soak the rice noodles for 1 hour in cold water. Push the garlic through a garlic press and stir-fry in the oil until golden brown, then discard the garlic.

Put the stock in a saucepan, add the coriander roots and stems, star anise and pepper and bring to the boil.

Add the fish sauce, soya sauce and sugar. Place the noodles and beansprouts in a sieve, immerse them in the boiling stock for 5 seconds, then divide them among 4 soup bowls. Repeat with the sliced beef, immersing it for 20 seconds. Divide the chopped coriander and spring onion (scallion) among the 4 bowls.

Pour the stock over the contents of the bowls and float the garlic oil on top.

SOUR & SPICY PRAWN SOUP

TomYam Koong

A beguilingly simple and attractive-looking soup with a clear stock base (for photograph, see page 2).

makes 4 bowls

4 small green chillies
2 coriander roots and stems
600ml/1 pint/2½ cups chicken stock
12 thin slivers galangal
2 stems lemongrass, finely chopped
4 kaffir lime leaves
8 small button mushrooms, quartered

8 king prawns, shelled, deveined and headless
  but with tail attached
2tbsp fish sauce
1½tbsp lemon juice
½tbsp Nam Prik Phao (see recipe on page 152)

FOR THE GARNISH
fresh coriander leaves for sprinkling

In a mortar, crush the green chillies with the coriander roots and stems.

Heat the stock to boiling point in a saucepan. Add the galangal, lemongrass, kaffir lime leaves and mushrooms and bring back to the boil.

Add the prawns, fish sauce, crushed chillies and coriander roots and stems, lemon juice and Nam Prik Phao and simmer for 1 minute.

Serve hot in individual soup bowls, allowing 2 prawns per person. Sprinkle with coriander leaves to serve.

VEGETARIAN SOUR & SPICY SOUP Ⓥ

TomYam Hed

makes 1 serving
(4 soup bowls full)

6 bird's eye chillies
1 litre/¾pint/4⅓ cups vegetable stock
12 thin slices galangal, thinly sliced
2 stems lemongrass, thinly sliced
200g/7oz button mushrooms, quartered
4 kaffir lime leaves
4 coriander roots and stems

pinch salt
1tsp sugar
2tbsp light soya sauce
2tbsp lemon juice

FOR THE GARNISH
fresh coriander leaves for sprinkling

Crush the chillies in a mortar.

Heat the stock in a pan. Put in the chillies, galangal, lemongrass, mushrooms, kaffir lime leaves and coriander roots and stems and bring to the boil.

Add the salt, sugar, soya sauce and lemon juice, then simmer for 2 minutes. Serve hot in soup bowls sprinkled with coriander.

VEGETABLE SOUP Ⓥ

Chiang Mai

As its name suggests, this soup is a tradition of northern Thailand. Quick and easy to make, it's an excellent standby recipe.

makes 4 bowls

40g/1 ½oz vermicelli
700ml/1 ¼ pints/3 cups vegetable stock
40g/1 ½oz cauliflower florets, finely sliced
40g/1 ½oz leek, finely sliced
60g/2oz mushrooms, finely sliced
40g/1 ½oz Chinese dried mushrooms, finely sliced
40g/1 ½oz celery heart, finely sliced

3 pieces baby corn, cut into thin rounds
1tbsp tapioca flour
4tsp light soya sauce
1tsp sugar
½tsp salt
pinch ground white pepper
sprinkling of fresh coriander leaves

Soak the vermicelli for 15 minutes in cold water and cut into pieces about 1.5cm/½in long.

Bring the vegetable stock to the boil in a saucepan and add the vegetables and the vermicelli. Return to the boil and simmer for 2 minutes.

Mix the tapioca flour with 2½tbsp water. Add the soya sauce, sugar, salt and pepper to the soup and thicken it with the dissolved tapioca flour. Stir in the fresh coriander leaves and remove from the heat. Serve the soup in bowls.

CHICKEN BALL SOUP WITH TOFU

Keang Jeud Tow Hu Look Chin Kai

makes 4 bowls

2 cloves garlic, peeled
1 coriander root and stem
150g/5oz raw minced chicken
¼tsp ground white pepper
1½tbsp potato flour
2tbsp light soya sauce
8 green asparagus spears, halved

600ml/1pint/2½ cups chicken stock
120g/4oz tofu, cut into small cubes
40g/1½oz carrot, cut into small cubes
60g/2oz watercress
15g/½oz fresh green peppercorns on
  the branch
1tsp fish sauce

In a mortar, pound the garlic with the coriander root and stem. Mix the chicken mince, garlic and coriander, pepper, potato flour and half the soya sauce together. Knead the mixture to make a dough and divide it into 16 small balls wrapped around the middle of the halved asparagus spears. Set aside.

Bring the chicken stock to the boil in a saucepan. Add the aparagus spears wrapped in the chicken mixture and simmer them for 2 minutes.

Add the tofu, carrots, watercress, green peppercorns, fish sauce and the rest of the soya sauce and simmer for another 2 minutes. Serve hot in soup bowls.

TOFU SOUP Ⓥ

Keang Jeud Tow Hu

makes 1 serving
(4 soup bowls full)

150g/5oz trimmed watercress
600ml/1 pint/2½ cups vegetable stock
200g/7oz tofu, cut into small cubes
15g/½oz fresh green peppercorns on the stem

100g/3½oz carrot, finely diced
1½tbsp light soya sauce
2tsp sugar

Remove thick stems from the watercress. (You should have 140g/5oz after trimming.) Heat the stock in a pan, add the tofu and simmer for 2 minutes. Add the watercress, green peppercorns, carrots, soya sauce and sugar and simmer for a further 2 minutes. Serve hot in soup bowls.

RIGHT: Chicken Ball Soup with Tofu

FLOATING MARKET

Po Teak

This a spectacular and substantial spicy seafood soup best served on its own as a starter.

makes 4 bowls

4 bird's eye chillies
2 coriander roots and stems
1 litre/1¾ pints/4⅓ cups chicken stock
12 thin slices galangal
2 stems lemongrass, thinly sliced
100g/3½oz mushrooms, quartered
4 kaffir lime leaves
80g/3oz fish fillet (4 pieces), cut into 2cm/¾in wide cubes
4 cherry tomatoes, halved
80g/3oz squid, cut into 2cm/¾in wide cubes
4 large prawns, shelled and deveined with tails left on

80g/3oz scallops
8 mussels in their shells
4 crab claws
5tbsp lemon juice
5tbsp fish sauce

FOR THE GARNISH
1tbsp Nam Prik Phao oil
  (see recipe on page 152)
fresh coriander leaves for sprinkling
10 Thai basil leaves

In a mortar, pound the chillies with the coriander roots and stems.

Put the chicken stock in a saucepan, bring to the boil, and add the galangal, lemongrass, mushrooms, kaffir lime leaves, chillies and coriander roots and stems. Bring to the boil and simmer for 5 minutes.

Add the fish fillets and simmer for 1 minute. Add the tomatoes, squid, prawns, scallops, mussels, crab claws, lemon juice and fish sauce. Simmer for 3 minutes.

Menam Chicken Soup

Tom Kha Kai

The basis of this soup, a gentle combination of chicken, coconut milk and lemongrass, is given heat and intensity with green chillies and flavourings (for photograph see detail on page 47). This is a soup to be eaten à la Thaie, served with the rest of the meal so that you can punctuate your enjoyment of other dishes with an occasional spoonful.

makes 4 bowls

400ml/14fl oz/1¾ cups chicken stock
400ml/14 fl oz/1¾ cups coconut milk
40g/1½oz galangal, finely sliced
1 stem lemongrass, finely sliced
4 kaffir lime leaves, crushed
200g/7oz boneless chicken breast with skin
   removed, cut into thin slices
80g/3oz mushrooms, quartered

5 green chillies, crushed
4tbsp fish sauce
4tbsp tamarind juice
2tbsp lemon juice
sprinkling of fresh coriander leaves
1tbsp oil of Nam Prik Phao
   (see recipe on page 152)

Put the stock in a saucepan and add the coconut milk. Bring to the boil over a medium heat and add the galangal, lemongrass and kaffir lime leaves.

Stir for 2 minutes, then add the chicken, mushrooms and crushed chillies. Simmer for 1 minute.

Add the fish sauce, tamarind and lemon juices. Bring back to the boil and stir in the coriander before removing from the heat. Transfer to soup bowls and float the oil of Nam Prik Phao on the surface. Serve hot.

Vegetarian Tofu Soup Ⓥ

Tom Kha Yod Phaeng

To make a vegetarian version of the above soup, use 25g/1oz deep-fried tofu instead of chicken and omit the chicken stock. Add 3½tbsp light soya sauce and omit the fish sauce.

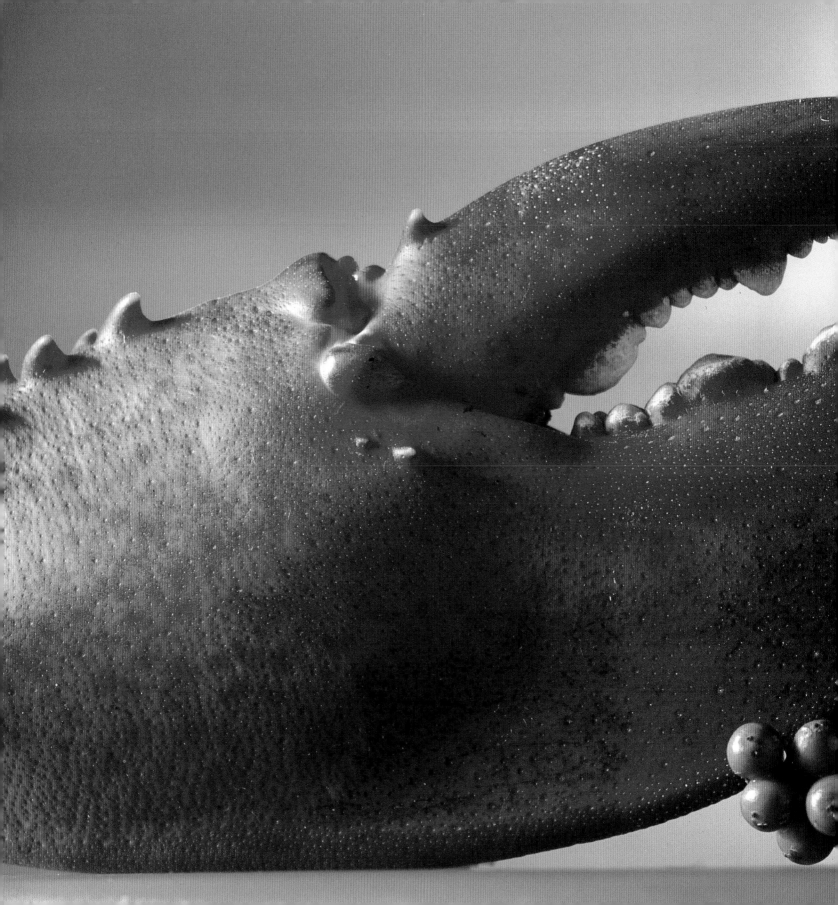

SEAFOOD

SALMON SOUFFLÉ

Homok Pla Isan

This light and delicious soufflé comes from the region of Isan in north-east Thailand.

makes 1 serving

30g/1oz sticky rice
2 cloves garlic, peeled
1 large red chilli
2.5cm/1in piece of galangal
2.5cm/1in piece lemongrass
250g/9oz fresh salmon, filleted
1tsp coconut milk
1½tbsp fish sauce

1tsp Red Curry Paste (see recipe on page 151)
1tsp sugar
2 shallots, finely sliced
5 stems dill, coarsely chopped
10 leaves lemon basil
1 banana leaf
4 toothpicks

Soak the sticky rice in cold water for 30 minutes, then pound into a paste in a mortar, or process.

Pound the garlic, chilli, galangal, and lemongrass together in a mortar, then mix with the rice.

Cut the salmon into fingers about 7cm/3in long without removing any skin, then gently mix them in a bowl with the pounded ingredients, adding the coconut milk, fish sauce, Red Curry Paste and sugar.

Stir in the shallots, dill and lemon basil, taking care not to break up the salmon fingers.

Cut 4 oval shapes about 23cm/9in long and 16cm/6in wide and 4 rectangles about 12 cm/4½in by 8cm/3in from the banana leaf, plus a strip about 27cm/11in long and 1.5cm/½in wide.

Place the rectangles lengthways over the ovals to give two thicknesses of banana leaf in the centre. Place a quarter of the mixture in the centre of each of the rectangles. Make a parcel with the banana leaves and fasten it at the top with the banana leaf strip and a toothpick.

Bring water to a fast boil in the bottom half of a steamer and steam the parcels for 12 minutes. Serve hot.

NOTE: This recipe may also be prepared with other firm-fleshed fish, such as cod, sole, monkfish or turbot.

IMPERIAL FISH

Pla Peaw Wan

This is a gentler version of Bangkok Fish (see recipe on page 73).

makes 1 serving

1½tbsp vegetable oil

40g/1½oz cucumber, quartered lengthways, deseeded and cut into thick triangular slices

3 pieces baby corn, quartered

2 button mushrooms, quartered

1 medium-sized tomato, cut into wedges

40g/1½oz mixed red, yellow and green bell peppers, sliced

1 slice Spanish onion

2tsp sliced root ginger, cut into julienne strips (matchsticks)

40g/1½oz pineapple, cubed

1 spring onion (scallion), cut into 3cm/1½in pieces

150ml/5fl oz/⅔ cup Sweet & Sour Sauce (see recipe on page 149)

200g/7oz cod, plaice, haddock or sole fillet

20g/¾oz flour

vegetable oil for deep-frying

FOR THE GARNISH

fresh coriander leaves for sprinkling

carved red radish flower (optional)

Heat the vegetable oil in a wok until very hot. Add all the vegetables and the pineapple and stir-fry for 30 seconds.

Add the Sweet & Sour Sauce and bring to the boil, then set aside and keep hot without allowing further cooking.

Coat the fish with the flour and deep-fry in oil heated to 180°C/350°F for about 5 minutes, until cooked. Drain it on absorbent paper, place it on a serving dish and cover with the vegetables and the sauce.

Sprinkle with the coriander leaves and decorate with the radish flower to serve.

FISH WITH CHILLI SAUCE

Sam Rod

makes 1 serving

150g/5oz pineapple, chopped
80g/3oz onion, chopped
40g/1½oz large red chilli, chopped
1 fingertip-size piece root ginger, chopped
4 cloves garlic, peeled and chopped
1 whole pomfret, sole, plaice, sea bass or trout,
  weighing about 500g/1lb 2oz
vegetable oil for deep-frying
1½tbsp vegetable oil
3½tbsp sugar

3tbsp tamarind juice
3tbsp fish sauce
2tbsp tapioca flour mixed with 3tbsp water
10 Thai basil leaves

FOR THE GARNISH
fresh coriander leaves for sprinkling
2 halved cucumber slices and 2 halved
  tomato slices

In a mortar or blender, crush together the pineapple, onion, chilli, ginger and garlic.

Deep-fry the fish in oil heated to 180°C/350°F for 10 minutes. Drain on absorbent paper.

Meanwhile, heat the vegetable oil in a wok until very hot. Add the crushed ingredients and stir-fry for 30 seconds.

Add the sugar, tamarind juice and fish sauce and simmer for 5 minutes.

Add the tapioca flour and water followed by the basil leaves, then remove from the heat.

Place the fish on a serving dish, coat with the sauce, sprinkle over the coriander leaves and garnish with the cucumber and tomato.

SCALLOPS FARANG

Hoy Shell Phad

This stir-fry is as pretty as a picture, the white scallops set against the colours of the lightly cooked vegetables.

makes 1 serving

20g/¾oz Chinese dried mushrooms
3tbsp vegetable oil
8 scallops, about 100g/3½oz
30g/1oz small broccoli florets
30g/1oz baby corn, quartered
30g/1oz button mushrooms, halved
½ celery stick, finely sliced
30g/1oz Spanish onion, finely sliced
1 piece medium-sized carrot, 4cm/1½in long,
  cut into julienne strips (matchsticks)

30g/1oz beansprouts
2tbsp oyster sauce
1tsp Blue Elephant Special Sauce
  (see recipe on page 152)

FOR THE GARNISH
fresh coriander leaves for sprinkling
carved red radish flower (optional)

Soak the Chinese mushrooms for 10 minutes in cold water and slice into small pieces.

Heat the oil in a wok until very hot. Add the scallops and stir-fry for 30 seconds.

Add all the vegetables and stir-fry for a further 2 minutes until half cooked.

Add the sauces and cook for a further 2 minutes.

Transfer to a serving dish, sprinkle with the coriander leaves and garnish with the radish flower.

STIR-FRIED SEAFOOD WITH GARLIC & PEPPERCORNS

Seafood Krathiam Prik Thai

The fresh green peppercorns add a spicy zest to this stir-fry.

makes 1 serving

4 cloves garlic, peeled
3tbsp vegetable oil
2 medium-sized prawns, shelled and deveined
70g/2½oz squid, cut into 2cm/¾in cubes
4 scallops
4 crab claws
pinch ground white pepper
1tbsp fish sauce
1tsp Blue Elephant Special Sauce
   (see recipe on page 152)

½tsp sugar
1½tbsp chicken stock
20g/¾oz fresh green peppercorns on the stem
1 stem fresh coriander, chopped

FOR THE GARNISH
green salad leaves
carved red radish flower (optional)

Pound the garlic in a mortar or push it through a garlic press.

Heat the oil in a wok until very hot. Add the garlic and, when it is golden-brown, add all the seafood and stir-fry for about 1 minute, until half-cooked.

Add the ground pepper, sauces, sugar and chicken stock, then simmer for 2 minutes.

Add the green peppercorns and coriander, then transfer to a serving dish lined on one side with the salad leaves. Garnish with the carved radish flower.

SWEET & SOUR PRAWNS

Kung Peaw Wan

A popular stir-fry, quickly and simply prepared.

makes 1 serving

2 tbsp vegetable oil
5 large prawns, shelled with tails left on, about
   150g/5oz
30g/1oz pineapple, cubed
1 tsp fresh root ginger
30g/1oz cucumber, quartered lengthways,
   deseeded and cut into thick triangular slices
½ a medium-sized tomato, cut into wedges
4 pieces baby corn, quartered
2 button mushrooms, quartered

30g/1oz mixed red, yellow and green bell
   peppers, sliced
1 slice Spanish onion
150ml/5fl oz/⅔ cup Sweet & Sour Sauce
   (see recipe on page 149)

FOR THE GARNISH
fresh coriander leaves for sprinkling
carved red radish flower (optional)

Heat the oil in a wok until very hot, add the prawns and stir-fry for 1 minute.

Add the pineapple, ginger and all the vegetables and stir-fry for a further 30 seconds.

Add the Sweet & Sour Sauce and bring to the boil, then transfer to a serving dish, sprinkle over the coriander leaves and garnish with the radish flower.

To make a vegetarian version of this recipe, see the recipe for Sweet & Sour Tofu on page 122.

PRAWN CURRY

Keang Curry Koong

Always a favourite dish, this prawn curry looks and tastes different from the norm – yellow and hot, with the heat mellowed by coconut milk.

makes 1 serving

2 cloves garlic, peeled
2 coriander roots and stems
2tbsp vegetable oil
2tsp Green Curry Paste
  (see recipe on page 151)
1½tsp curry powder
1tsp ground turmeric
300ml/10fl oz/1¼ cups coconut milk
1tsp sugar
1tbsp fish sauce
1tbsp unsweetened condensed milk

1 spring onion (scallion), cut into 2cm/¾in
  pieces
60g/2oz onion, very finely sliced
5 medium-sized prawns, shelled and deveined
  with tails left on, about 100g/3¾oz
7cm/3in length of celery taken from the heart,
  with leaves, very finely sliced

FOR THE GARNISH
1½tbsp cream of coconut milk
fresh coriander leaves for sprinkling

In a mortar, pound the garlic with the coriander roots and stems.

Heat the oil in a wok until very hot. Add the Green Curry Paste, garlic and coriander and stir-fry for about 3 minutes until an aroma develops.

Add the curry powder and ground turmeric. Add the coconut milk, bring to the boil, then add the sugar, fish sauce and condensed milk. Simmer for 5 minutes.

Add the spring onion, onion, prawns and celery, then simmer for 30 seconds.

Transfer to a serving dish, float the cream of coconut milk on top of the curry and sprinkle with the coriander leaves.

STEAMED FISH WITH LIME

Pla Neung Manao

A delightfully simple recipe, the sauce, with its mirepoix of finely diced raw vegetables is reminiscent of modern French cuisine. However, the perfume of lemongrass and the presence of chillies and coriander firmly identify the dish as Thai.

makes 1 serving

2 stems lemongrass
1 whole fish such as sea bass, mullet, trout or
    sole, weighing about 500g/1lb 2oz
4 cloves garlic, peeled and very finely diced
15g/½oz carrot, peeled and very finely diced
4 coriander stems, very finely chopped
6 bird's eye chillies, finely sliced
2tsp sugar

3tbsp fish sauce
4½tbsp lime juice

FOR THE GARNISH
green salad leaves
5 lime slices
fresh coriander branches

Crush the lemongrass in a mortar. Score the fish with diagonal cuts on both sides. Place it on a steaming tray on a bed of the crushed lemongrass and steam over boiling water for about 15–20 minutes until cooked.

In a bowl, combine the garlic and carrot with the remaining ingredients for the sauce.

To serve, arrange the salad leaves on one side of a serving dish and place the fish beside them. Pour the sauce evenly over the fish and place the lime slices and coriander branches on top.

PRAWNS WITH RED CURRY SAUCE

Chuchi Koong

The uncompromisingly hot yet subtly flavoured sauce to go with these deep-fried prawns can be made in a wok in 5 minutes.

makes 1 serving

1½tbsp dried shrimps
8 medium-sized prawns, shelled and deveined
  with heads left on
vegetable oil for deep-frying
1½tbsp vegetable oil
3tbsp Red Curry Paste (see recipe on
  page 151)
150ml/5fl oz/⅔ cup coconut milk
2tbsp sugar

1tbsp fish sauce
1 kaffir lime leaf, finely sliced

FOR THE GARNISH
green salad leaves
1 Chinese cabbage leaf, finely sliced
10 Thai basil leaves
1½tbsp cream of coconut milk
fresh coriander leaves for sprinkling

Pound the dried shrimps in a mortar. Deep-fry the prawns in oil heated to 180°C/350°F for 1 minute, drain on absorbent paper, set aside and keep hot.

Heat the oil in a wok until very hot. Add the Red Curry Paste and stir-fry for about 3 minutes until an aroma develops.

Add the coconut milk and bring it to the boil.

Add the dried shrimps, sugar and fish sauce. Stir-fry for 5 seconds.

Add the kaffir lime leaf, then remove from the heat.

Arrange the prawns in a serving dish on a bed of salad leaves sprinkled with the sliced Chinese cabbage. Put the basil leaves on top of the prawns and cover with the contents of the wok. Pour over the cream of coconut milk, then sprinkle with the coriander leaves.

SEAFOOD SALAD

Yam Talay

You can add glamour to this dish with its tasty dressing by serving it on scallop shells.

makes 1 serving

2 cloves garlic, peeled
1 large red chilli
1 bird's eye chilli
40g/1½oz squid, cut into 2cm/¾in cubes
1 large prawn
2 medium-sized prawns with head
4 scallops
4 mussels with half shells
2 crab claws
½tsp sugar
2½tbsp fish sauce
2½tbsp lemon juice

1 stem lemongrass, finely sliced
2 kaffir lime leaves, finely sliced
30g/1oz red onion, finely sliced
1 spring onion (scallion), finely sliced
1 piece medium-sized carrot, about 4cm/1½in long, cut into julienne strips (matchsticks)
5 mint leaves
3 stems coriander leaves chopped

FOR THE GARNISH
green salad leaves

In a mortar, pound the garlic into a paste with the chillies.

Bring a pan of water to the boil, then add the seafood. Boil for about 1 minute.

Drain the seafood well and put into a bowl. Mix in the chilli and garlic paste, sugar, fish sauce and lemon juice.

Add the remaining ingredients and toss lightly, then place on a serving dish on a bed of green salad leaves. Serve cool but not chilled.

BANGKOK FISH

Pla Rad Phrik

*The cachet of this famous dish is in its sauce. Hot, spicy, sweet and gingery,
it is packed with al dente vegetables – a true classic.*

makes 4 servings

75g/2½oz red chilli
40g/1½oz cloves garlic, peeled
150g/5oz fresh pineapple
1½tbsp root ginger, peeled and diced
40g/1½oz Spanish onion
800g/1lb 12oz firm, large-flaked fish fillets, such
  as cod, monkfish or turbot
2½tbsp flour
3tbsp vegetable oil
120g/4½oz sugar
6tbsp fish sauce

8tbsp tamarind juice
40g/1½oz each red, yellow and green bell
  peppers, sliced fairly thickly
4 spring onions (scallion),
  cut into 3cm/1½in lengths
vegetable oil for deep-frying

FOR THE GARNISH
fresh coriander leaves for sprinkling
carved red radish flower (optional)

Coarsely grind or process the chilli with the garlic. Crush the pineapple into a pulp. (If you
use canned pineapple, reduce the quantity of sugar in the recipe to compensate for the syrup.)

In a mortar, pound the ginger to make a paste (it will keep for up to three days in a
refrigerator.) Slice half the Spanish onion finely.

Make an onion paste with the remainder of the Spanish onion in the same way as the ginger
paste. Onion, however, should be used straight away.

Coat the fish fillets with the flour, then set aside.

Heat the oil in a wok until very hot, then add the garlic and chilli. Stir-fry for 5 seconds.
Add the pineapple pulp, ginger and onion pastes and stir-fry for a further 5 seconds.

Add the sugar, fish sauce and tamarind juice and simmer for 2 minutes. Add all the
vegetables and stir-fry for 3 minutes. Set aside and keep hot, without allowing the mixture
to continue cooking.

Deep-fry the fish for about 5 minutes, until it is cooked, then transfer to a serving dish. Pour
the contents of the wok over it. Garnish with the coriander leaves and a carved radish flower.

SEAFOOD PHUKET-STYLE

Seafood Phad Nam Prik Phao

The island of Phuket is renowned for its seafood. Chilli-rich Nam Prik Phao Sauce (see recipe on page 152) gives this dish a spicy kick.

makes 1 serving

2tbsp vegetable oil
2tbsp Nam Prik Phao Sauce (see recipe on page 152)
1 medium-sized prawn, shelled and deveined with tail left on
1 large prawn, shelled and deveined with head left on
4 mussels
4 scallops
4 crab claws
30g/1oz squid, cut into 2cm/¾in cubes
1 stick celery, sliced
30g/1oz mixed red, yellow and green bell peppers, sliced

1 piece medium-sized carrot, about 4cm/1½in long, cut into julienne strips (matchsticks)
1½tbsp Blue Elephant Special Sauce (see recipe on page 152)
1tbsp oyster sauce
1tsp sugar
5 Thai basil leaves

FOR THE GARNISH
green salad leaves
fresh coriander leaves for sprinkling

Heat the oil in a wok until very hot. Add the Nam Prik Phao Sauce and stir-fry for 5 seconds. Add all the seafood and stir-fry for about 2 minutes until it is almost cooked.

Add all the vegetables, the sauces, sugar and 3tbsp water, then stir-fry for a further 1 minute.

Mix in the basil leaves, then transfer to a serving dish lined with salad leaves. Sprinkle over the coriander leaves to serve.

STEAMED FISH BLUE ELEPHANT

PlaYai Blue Elephant

There is nothing like steaming to preserve the delicate taste of fresh fish and nothing like the simply prepared sauce of this recipe to complement it.

makes 1 serving

FOR THE SAUCE
2tbsp soya bean paste
1 slice Spanish onion
15g/½oz fresh ginger
2 cloves garlic
pinch ground white pepper
1tbsp light soya sauce
1½tsp oyster sauce
2tbsp vegetable oil

30g/1oz vermicelli
1 whole fish such as red or grey mullet, sea bass or trout, weighing about 500g/1lb 2oz
5 pieces baby corn, quartered
7 button mushrooms, quartered
1 stick celery, sliced

1 spring onion (scallion), sliced
5 thin strips red bell pepper, sliced
2 black mushrooms, sliced
30g/1oz Spanish onion, sliced
30g/1oz Chinese cabbage, finely sliced
1 small marble-sized piece fresh ginger, cut into julienne strips (matchsticks)
3 stems peppercorns
2tsp Blue Elephant Special Sauce (see recipe on page 152)
1tbsp oyster sauce

FOR THE GARNISH
4 slices cucumber
2 lemon wedges

Mince, mix or process all the sauce ingredients together and set aside.

Soak the vermicelli in cold water for 15 minutes, and cut into 8cm/3in strips.

Score the fish deeply with diagonal cuts on both sides. Smear it with the prepared sauce, ensuring that some enters the cuts and the stomach cavity.

Place the fish on a steaming tray. Put the vegetables, peppecorns and vermicelli over the fish and season with the Blue Elephant Special Sauce and oyster sauce.

Steam over boiling water for about 15-20 minutes, until the fish is cooked, then transfer to a serving dish with the vegetables and vermicelli. Garnish with the cucumber slices and lemon wedges.

GINGER LOBSTER

Lobster Jien

A splendid gingery and peppery stir-fry to go with lobster simply boiled in a bouillon. (For photograph see detail on page 57.)

makes 1 serving

FOR THE BOUILLON
30g/1oz celery, coarsely chopped
30g/1oz onion, coarsely chopped
30g/1oz leek, coarsely chopped
10 black peppercorns

1 fresh, uncooked lobster, about 600g/1lb 2oz
20g/¾oz unsalted butter
60g/2oz minced chicken
6tbsp chicken stock
40g/1½oz root ginger, cut into julienne strips
   (matchsticks)
3 Chinese black mushrooms, finely chopped
30g/1oz Spanish onion, finely chopped

1 spring onion (scallion), cut into
   2cm/¾in pieces
2 branches fresh green peppercorns
pinch ground white pepper
2tbsp Blue Elephant Special Sauce (see recipe
   on page 152)
1½tbsp oyster sauce
¼tsp tapioca flour dissolved in 1tsp water

FOR THE GARNISH
1 leek, 1 stick celery and 1 large red chilli, cut
   into julienne strips (matchsticks)
fresh coriander leaves for sprinkling

Chop the bouillon ingredients coarsely. Put the bouillon ingredients into 2 litres/3½ pints/ 8¾ cups water and bring to the boil. Boil for 5 minutes, then immerse the lobster. Boil for a further 8 minutes.

Remove the lobster, halve it lengthways with a sharp knife and place it on a serving dish. Keep hot.

Heat the butter in a wok until the froth has almost disappeared from the surface. Add the minced chicken and chicken stock, then stir-fry for about 3 minutes, until it is cooked.

Add the ginger, mushrooms, onion, spring onion (scallion), green peppercorns, ground white pepper, Blue Elephant Special Sauce and oyster sauce. Stir-fry for 1 minute.

Stir in the dissolved tapioca flour.

Coat the lobster with the contents of the wok and garnish with the julienned leek, celery and chilli and coriander leaves.

POULTRY

GINGER CHICKEN

Kai Phad Khing

Ginger has always been considered a powerful aphrodisiac in Thailand, and this delicate combination of stir-fried chicken and shredded ginger is no exception.

makes 1 serving

FOR THE MARINADE
1 clove garlic, peeled
½tsp light soy sauce
2 pinches ground white pepper

150g/5oz chicken breast, cut into 1cm/2.5in thick slices
3tbsp vegetable oil
3½tbsp chicken stock
20g/¾oz ginger, cut into julienne strips (matchsticks)
30g/1oz Spanish onion, sliced
4 black mushrooms, sliced

60g/2oz mixed red, green and yellow bell peppers, sliced
4 button mushrooms, quartered
1 spring onion (scallion), cut into 2cm/¾in pieces
1½tbsp oyster sauce
1tsp Blue Elephant Special Sauce (see recipe on page 152)

FOR THE GARNISH
fresh coriander leaves for sprinkling
carved red radish flower (optional)

To make the marinade, crush the garlic and mix it with the soy sauce and pepper. Coat the chicken with the marinade and set aside for 15 minutes.

Heat the oil in a wok until very hot. Add the chicken slices and stir-fry for about 2 minutes until half-cooked.

Add all the vegetables and the chicken stock and stir-fry for 30 seconds, then add the sauces and cook for a further 2 minutes until the chicken is done.

Transfer to a serving dish, sprinkle with the coriander leaves and garnish with the radish flower. Serve hot.

EMERALD CHICKEN

Kai Ho Bai Toey

Green toey leaves make a most attractive parcel for marinated chicken legs in this fairly simple deep-fry recipe.

makes 1 serving

FOR THE MARINADE
3 cloves garlic, peeled
5 coriander roots and stems
½ toey leaf, very finely chopped
4tbsp oyster sauce
2tbsp barbecue sauce
1tsp ground white pepper
2½tbsp light soya sauce
2tsp sugar

4 boneless chicken thighs weighing about
   600g/1¼lb
8 whole toey leaves, 30cm/1ft long
2 bamboo sticks, 20cm/8in long
vegetable oil for deep-frying
Sesame Sauce (see recipe on page 150)
   to serve

FOR THE GARNISH
green salad leaves

In a mortar, pound the garlic into a paste together with the coriander roots and stems. Mix all the marinade ingredients together in a bowl and marinate the chicken for 30 minutes.

Wrap each chicken thigh in a toey leaf. Skewer 4 pieces on each bamboo stick, securing the toey leaf wrapping by piercing the tip.

Deep-fry in oil heated to 180°C/350°F for 10–15 minutes until cooked. Remove and drain on absorbent paper. Transfer to a serving dish lined with salad leaves and serve hot.

Serve with Sesame Sauce separately in a bowl.

CASHEW CHICKEN

Kai Himmapan

The flavour of this classic stir-fry is given a uniquely Thai lift.

makes 1 serving

FOR THE MARINADE
1 clove garlic, peeled
½tsp light soy sauce
2 pinches ground white pepper

1½tbsp cashew nuts
vegetable oil
150g/5oz chicken breast, skinned and cut into
    1cm/½in thick slices
2tbsp chicken stock
20g/¾oz Spanish onion, sliced
60g/2oz mixed red, green and yellow bell
    peppers, sliced

1 piece of a medium-sized carrot, about
    3cm/1¼in long, cut into julienne strips
    (matchsticks)
2 pieces baby corn, quartered
4 button mushrooms, quartered
1 spring onion (scallion), cut into 2cm/¾in
    pieces
30g/1oz pineapple, cut into small pieces
1½tbsp oyster sauce
1½tsp Blue Elephant Special Sauce
    (see recipe on page 152)

FOR THE GARNISH
coriander leaves for sprinkling
carved red radish flower (optional)

To make the marinade, crush the garlic and mix it with the soy sauce and pepper. Coat the chicken with the marinade and set aside for 15 minutes.

Fry the cashew nuts briefly in a small amount of oil until slightly browned. Heat 3tbsp oil in a wok until very hot. Add the chicken and stir-fry for 1 minute until the chicken is half cooked.

Add all the vegetables and the stock and the pineapple and stir-fry for 30 seconds. Add the sauces and cook for a further 1 minute, until the chicken is cooked through.

Mix in the cashew nuts. Transfer to a serving dish. Sprinkle over the coriander leaves and decorate with the radish flower. Serve hot.

To make a vegetarian version of this recipe, replace the chicken breast with 80g/3oz ready deep-fried tofu cubes. Reduce the amount of vegetable oil to 2tbsp, omit the oyster sauce and add 1tsp light soya sauce.

THAI CHICKEN SOUFFLÉ

Homok Kai

Steaming ingredients wrapped in a banana leaf is a popular cooking method and making the cups for this recipe is really not very difficult. The spiciness of the chicken filling is tempered with coconut milk. (For photograph see detail on page 79.)

makes 4 pieces

1 banana leaf
8 toothpicks, cut in half

FOR THE FILLING
75g/2½oz minced chicken
½tsp finely sliced kaffir lime rind
1 piece krachai root, about 7.5cm/3in long,
   finely sliced
1 coriander root and stem
20g/¾oz shallot
pinch ground white pepper
1 clove garlic, peeled
1tbsp fish sauce
2tsp sugar
1 kaffir lime leaf, finely sliced

200ml/7fl oz coconut milk
2tbsp Red Curry Paste
   (see recipe on page 151)
½ large egg

TO LINE THE BOTTOM OF THE BANANA CUPS
20 basil leaves
20g/¾oz thinly sliced chicken

FOR THE GARNISH
green salad leaves
3tbsp cream of coconut milk
1 red chilli, finely sliced

Make 4 banana cups, securing each one with a short piece of toothpick or use small soup bowls (7cm/2¾in diameter) instead.

Process all the filling ingredients until they form a homogenous mixture.

Place a little kaffir lime leaf, some basil leaves and a thin slice of chicken at the bottom of each banana cup and pour over the filling, dividing it equally among the cups. Top with the cream of coconut milk and sprinkle over the finely sliced red chilli.

Bring water to a fast boil in a steamer, place the banana cups on the upper section and steam for 12 to 15 minutes.

Transfer the banana cups to a serving dish lined with the green salad leaves.

For a vegetarian version of this recipe, see page 128.

STUFFED CHICKEN WINGS

Pik Kai Sod Sai

Although it is fairly tricky to make, this is a wonderful titbit!

makes 4 pieces

100g/3oz self-raising flour
4 chicken wings
vegetable oil for deep-frying

FOR THE FILLING
20g/¾oz vermicelli
100g/3½oz minced chicken
1tbsp Blue Elephant Special Sauce (see recipe
  on page 152)
1tbsp light soya sauce
1tsp ground white pepper
1tsp sugar

1½tbsp vegetable oil
150g/5oz mushrooms, finely sliced
20g/¾oz cauliflower, finely sliced
15g/½oz white cabbage, finely sliced
1 stick celery, finely sliced
20g/¾oz Spanish onion, finely sliced
Red Chilli Sweet & Sour Sauce to serve
  (see recipe on page 146)

FOR THE GARNISH
green salad leaves

Mix the self-raising flour with 150ml/5fl oz/⅔ cup water to make a batter, then set aside.

Soak the vermicelli for 15 minutes in cold water, then cut into 5cm/2in lengths.

To make the filling, mix the minced chicken in a bowl, with the sauces, pepper, sugar and oil. Knead well, then mix in the vermicelli. Add the vegetables and mix lightly. Set aside.

Debone the chicken wings, clean well and remove any feathers.

Hold a chicken wing between the thumb and forefinger and spoon ¼ of the filling into the cavity. Press down lightly so that the filling is firm, then fold the flap of skin over the top to seal.

Heat deep-frying oil to 180°C/350°F and, holding a chicken wing by the tip, dip it into the prepared batter then, using a pair of kitchen tongs, into the frying oil, retaining it for a few seconds and then gently releasing it. Repeat with the remaining wings. Deep-fry the wings for about 7 minutes until golden-brown. (When the wings rise to the surface of the oil they are done.) Remove and drain on absorbent paper.

Transfer to a dish lined with green salad leaves and serve immediately. Serve Red Chilli Sweet & Sour Sauce separately in a bowl.

MADAME PA'S CHICKEN CURRY

Keaw Wan Kai

One of the most popular Thai dishes, this green curry is given a special lift by The Blue Elephant's curry chef, Madame Pa.

makes 1 serving

1 cup fresh coriander leaves
3tbsp vegetable oil
1½tbsp green curry paste
pinch freshly ground coriander seeds
1 pinch freshly ground cumin seeds
370ml/13fl oz/1½ cups coconut milk
1 boned and skinned chicken breast, sliced into
  bite-size pieces
2 green aubergines (eggplants), quartered
sprig pea aubergines (eggplants)

1tsp sugar
1½tbsp fish sauce
2 kaffir lime leaves, torn in half
6 Thai basil leaves
½ fresh red chilli, thinly sliced

FOR THE GARNISH
2tsp cream of coconut milk
fresh Thai basil for sprinkling

In a mortar, pound the fresh coriander leaves.

Heat the oil in a wok or saucepan until very hot. Add the pounded coriander leaves and fry for 1 minute. Add the curry paste, coriander and cumin, and stir-fry for about 2 minutes until an aroma develops. Lower the heat and add the coconut milk a little at a time. Allow it to simmer for about 2 minutes, then add the chicken and cook until cooked through.

Add the green aubergines (eggplants) and pea aubergines (eggplants), sugar, fish sauce, kaffir lime, basil leaves and chilli. Simmer for 5 minutes. Transfer the curry to a clay pot or tureen, float the cream of coconut milk on top and sprinkle with the Thai basil.

VEGETARIAN GREEN CURRY Ⓥ

Keaw Wan Jay

To make a vegetarian version of this recipe, substitute the chicken with 50g/2oz tofu. Add 25g/1oz small broccoli florets and 4 pieces baby corn, cut in 4 lengthways. Use light soya sauce instead of fish sauce and prepare the dish as above.

CHICKEN & PRAWN IN A NEST

Rung Nok

makes 1 serving
(2 pieces)

FOR THE POTATO BASKET
120g/4oz potatoes
2tsp tapioca flour
vegetable oil for deep-frying

FOR THE FILLING
100g/3½oz spring greens (mock seaweed),
  very finely shredded
8 quail's eggs
1tsp tapioca flour
2tsp vegetable oil
1 clove garlic, crushed
120g/4oz boiled and skinned chicken breast, diced
40g/1½oz medium-sized prawns, shelled,
  deveined and chopped
pinch ground white pepper

3tbsp chicken stock
1tsp Dark Soya Sauce
2tsp oyster sauce
1tsp Blue Elephant Special Sauce
  (see recipe on page 152)
very small quantities, less than 10g/¼oz, of each
  of the following:
carrot, diced
water chestnut, diced
mixed red, yellow and green bell peppers, diced
1½tbsp sweetcorn kernels
1½tbsp green peas, shelled

FOR THE GARNISH
fresh coriander leaves for sprinkling
carved red radish flower (optional)

To make the basket, grate the potato and mix with tapioca flour. Line a 14cm/6in diameter sieve with the potato strips, then take a second sieve of the same size and press down over the potato strips to hold them in place. Immerse the two sieves in oil heated to 180°C/350°F and deep-fry for about 2 to 3 minutes until the potato is golden-brown. Remove from the oil, carefully detach the potato basket from the sieves and set aside to drain on absorbent paper.

Deep-fry the spring greens for about 3 seconds until crisp, then set aside to drain on absorbent paper.

Boil the quail's eggs for 5 minutes, remove the shells, then deep-fry them for 1 minute. Dissolve the tapioca flour in 2tsp water.

Heat the oil in a wok until very hot. Add the garlic and let it take colour, then stir-fry the chicken and the prawns for 3 minutes. Add the pepper, chicken stock and sauces. Mix well and add the vegetables, continuing to mix until the ingredients come to the boil. Add the eggs and the tapioca dissolved in water. Mix and remove from the heat.

Lay the deep-fried spring green leaves on the serving dish to form a base and place the potato basket on it. Fill the basket with the stir-fried mixture, sprinkle with fresh coriander leaves and garnish with a radish flower.

Tuk's Duck Salad

Laab Ped

Tuk, expert salad chef at The Blue Elephant in London, devised this meaty and very spicy dish.

makes 1 serving

FOR THE PASTE
40g/1½oz shallots
5 cloves garlic, peeled
20g/¾oz galangal
1 stem lemongrass
4 dried red chillies

100g/5oz duck breast
1tsp sugar
2tbsp fish sauce
2tbsp lemon juice
1½tbsp glutinous rice, roasted and ground

2 pinches small dried chillies, roasted and ground or ground chilli powder
2tbsp finely sliced red onion
2 spring onions (scallion), finely sliced
6 mint leaves
1 sprig Thai parsley

FOR THE GARNISH
sprinklings of fried, sliced shallot
fried small dried red chilli
fresh coriander leaves
green salad leaves

To make the paste, roast the shallots, garlic, galangal, lemongrass and red chillies on a baking tray in a very hot oven for 4 minutes. Pound together in a mortar and set aside.

Grill the duck breast under a very hot grill for about 5 minutes until half cooked, turning it over after 2½ minutes, then cut into thin slices.

Put the prepared paste in a pan, then add 3tbsp water and the duck slices. Mix together and stir-fry for 5 minutes.

Remove the pan from the heat and stir in the sugar, fish sauce and fresh lemon juice. Add the rice and chilli powder, then fold in the red onion, spring onions, mint leaves and parsley.

Garnish one side of a serving dish with salad leaves. Arrange the sliced duck salad on the other side of the dish and sprinkle with the fried shallot and chilli and the fresh coriander leaves.

Tuk's Vegetarian Salad ⓥ

To make a vegetarian version of this recipe, substitute 100g/3½oz ready deep-fried tofu cubes for the duck and the same quantity of light soya sauce for the fish sauce.

DUCK WITH TAMARIND SAUCE

Ped Makarm

*The rich, special sweet-and-sour tamarind sauce makes a perfect
complement to lightly cooked breast of duck.*

makes 1 serving

180g/6oz lean breast of duck (magret)

FOR THE MARINADE
1tsp coriander seeds
1 piece star anise
2.5cm/1in cinnamon stick
1 clove garlic, peeled
1 coriander root and stem
2tsp Blue Elephant Special Sauce
    (see recipe on page 152)

FOR THE SAUCE
180g/6oz palm sugar
2tsp fish sauce
120ml/4fl oz/½ cup light soya sauce
250ml/8fl oz/1 cup tamarind sauce
    (see recipe on page 148)
3tbsp tapioca flour

FOR THE GARNISH
1tsp deep-fried sliced shallots
1tsp deep-fried large dried chilli
2tbsp spring greens (mock seaweed), deep-fried
green salad leaves

To make the marinade, dry-roast the coriander seed, star anise and cinnamon. Pound them with the garlic and coriander root and stem in a mortar. Mix in The Blue Elephant Special Sauce and marinate the duck breast with the mixture for at least 1 hour, preferably overnight.

For the deep-fried garnishes (taking larger quantities and storing the remainder in airtight containers for subsequent use), heat the oil to 180°C/350°F. Deep-fry the sliced shallots for about 2 minutes until golden-brown. Cut the chilli into 1cm/½in pieces and dip it briefly into the hot oil. Slice the spring greens finely and deep-fry for a few moments only, until crisp. When removed from the oil all these items should be drained on absorbent paper.

To make the sauce, bring 3½tbsp water to the boil and dissolve the palm sugar in it. Add the fish sauce and soya sauce and return to the boil. Add the tamarind sauce and simmer for 2 minutes. Meanwhile, dissolve the tapioca flour in 1tbsp water. Add to the sauce and mix well until it thickens. Set aside and keep hot.

Grill the duck breast under a very hot grill for about 4 minutes on each side, until half cooked. Garnish one side of a serving dish with salad leaves. On the other side, make a bed of deep-fried mock seaweed. Cut the duck into slices and place, overlapping evenly, on the seaweed. Coat with the sauce and sprinkle over the fried shallot and chilli garnish.

GRILLED DUCK CURRY

Kaeng Phed Ped Yang

Highly spiced and coconut flavoured, fruit tempers the heat of this classic and not difficult to prepare curry.

makes 1 serving

150g/5oz duck breast (magret)
5 grapes
2 cloves garlic, peeled
2 coriander roots and stems
2 tsp vegetable oil
1½tbsp Red Curry Paste (see recipe on page 151)
pinch ground coriander seeds
pinch ground cumin seeds
250ml/8fl oz/1 cup coconut milk
1 tbsp fish sauce
1½tbsp sugar (reduce amount if using canned pineapple)

2 kaffir lime leaves, finely sliced
40g/1½oz pineapple, preferably fresh, cut into small pieces
2 cherry tomatoes, halved
12 Thai basil leaves
½ large red chilli, sliced

FOR THE GARNISH
2tsp cream of coconut milk
fresh basil leaves for sprinkling

Grill the duck under a very hot grill for about 4 minutes on each side, until it is half cooked. Slice and set aside.

Remove the seeds from the grapes, if any. In a mortar, pound the garlic with the coriander roots and stems.

Heat the oil in a wok until very hot. Add the Red Curry Paste, pounded garlic and coriander and the ground coriander and cumin. Stir-fry for about 3 minutes, until an aroma develops.

Add the coconut milk a little at a time and bring to the boil. Add the fish sauce, sugar and kaffir lime leaves, simmer for 5 minutes, then add the duck.

Add the grapes, the pineapple and the cherry tomatoes and simmer for a further 1 minute. Add the Thai basil leaves and the red chilli. Transfer to a serving pot, float the cream of coconut milk on top of the curry and sprinkle with basil leaves.

To make a vegetarian version of this recipe using tofu instead of duck, see page 125.

MEAT

LAMB CURRY

Massaman Kae

This classic Thai curry originated in the South. Every Thai cook has his or her individual variation of which the family recipe below is authentic and succulent.

makes 1 serving

1 clove garlic, peeled
1 sliver ginger root
2 coriander roots with stems
vegetable oil for deep-frying
250g/8oz lean roasting lamb, cut into cubes
    about 2.5cm/1in wide
1 medium-sized potato, quartered
3tbsp vegetable oil
3tbsp Massaman Curry Paste
  (see recipe on page 153)
1 bayleaf
pinch ground cinnamon
pinch ground coriander seeds

pinch ground cardamom
250ml/8fl oz/1 cup coconut milk
3 whole shallots
3tbsp palm sugar
3tbsp fish sauce
4tbsp tamarind juice

FOR THE GARNISH
15g/½oz cashew nuts, fried in oil for a few
    seconds
2tsp cream of coconut milk
fresh coriander leaves for sprinkling

Coarsely mince or process the garlic with the ginger and coriander roots and stems.

Deep-fry the lamb in very hot oil (180°C/350°F) for 5 minutes. Remove the lamb, then deep-fry the potato pieces for 10 minutes.

Heat the vegetable oil in a wok or saucepan until very hot. Add the Massaman Curry Paste, ginger, garlic, coriander roots and stems, bayleaf and ground spices.

Stir-fry for about 5 minutes, until an aroma develops. Add the coconut milk, meat, potato and shallots. Bring to a boil.

Add the sugar and fish sauce. Simmer for 10 minutes, adding up to 4tbsp tamarind juice and 5tbsp water until the sauce has a medium consistency.

Transfer to a serving pot or tureen, add the fried cashew nuts, float the cream of coconut milk on top and sprinkle with the coriander leaves.

CHILLIED LAMB

Kae Phad Phrik

Vegetables temper the powerful spiciness of this creative Blue Elephant twist on a simply prepared Thai curry.

makes 1 serving

1 Spanish onion, sliced
2 red chillies
2 cloves garlic, peeled
1 tsp Red Curry Paste (see recipe on page 151)
3 tbsp vegetable oil
150g/5oz lean roasting leg of lamb, cut into
    3mm/$\frac{1}{10}$in slices
40g/1$\frac{1}{2}$oz green aubergine (eggplant),
    quartered
60g/2oz mixed red, green and yellow bell
    peppers, sliced
20g/$\frac{3}{4}$oz baby aubergine (eggplant)

1$\frac{1}{2}$tbsp coconut milk
1$\frac{1}{2}$tbsp fresh green peppercorns
1 tsp sugar
1 tbsp fish sauce
2 tsp Blue Elephant Special Sauce
    (see recipe on page 152)
6 Thai basil leaves

FOR THE GARNISH
fresh coriander leaves for sprinkling
carved red radish flower (optional)

In a mortar, pound 60g/2oz Spanish onion, the chillies, garlic and Red Curry Paste, or process together.

Heat the oil in a wok until very hot, then stir-fry the pounded ingredients for 30 seconds. Add the lamb and stir-fry for a further 1 minute. Then add all the vegetables and cook for 2 minutes.

Add the coconut milk, 3tbsp water and all the remaining ingredients except for the basil leaves. Mix well, then toss in the basil, stir it into the mixture and remove from the heat.

Transfer to a serving dish, sprinkle over the coriander leaves, garnish with the radish flower and serve hot.

PORK WITH GREEN PEPPERCORNS

Mou Phad Kraphaw Prik Thai Sod

It's worth seeking out the fresh peppercorns to make this dish.

makes 1 serving

2 cloves garlic, peeled
1 large red chilli
¼ Spanish onion
1tsp Red Curry Paste (see recipe on page 151)
2 bird's eye chillies, finely sliced
3tbsp vegetable oil
200g/7oz lean pork, minced
1 kaffir lime leaf
1½tbsp fresh green peppercorns
10 sweet basil leaves

2tsp Blue Elephant Special Sauce
  (see recipe on page 152)
1½tsp fish sauce
pinch sugar

FOR THE GARNISH
green salad leaves
fresh coriander leaves for sprinkling
carved red radish flower (optional)

In a mortar, pound the garlic with the red chilli, onion and Red Curry Paste.

Heat the oil in a wok until very hot and stir-fry the pounded ingredients and the bird's eye chillies for 30 seconds.

Add the minced pork and cook for a further 2 minutes.

Add the kaffir lime leaf, green peppercorns and basil leaves and stir-fry for 5 seconds. Add the remaining ingredients and 3tbsp water, then mix them in.

Transfer to a serving dish lined with salad leaves, sprinkle with coriander, garnish with a radish flower and serve hot.

(This recipe may also be prepared with chicken instead of pork.)

SWEET MELODY

Mou Peaw Wan

A perennially popular sweet-and-sour dish of pork and al dente vegetables, this is basically a quick and easy stir-fry. If you need to use canned pineapple in syrup instead of fresh, reduce the amount of Sweet & Sour Sauce slightly to compensate.

makes 1 serving

3tbsp vegetable oil

150g/5oz lean, boneless pork, sliced and cut into bite-size pieces

40g/1½oz cucumber, quartered, deseeded and cut into thick slices

60g/2oz tomato, cut into wedges

40g/1½oz mixed red, yellow and green bell peppers, sliced

¼ Spanish onion, sliced

3 pieces baby corn, quartered

2 button mushrooms, quartered

40g/1½oz pineapple, cut into pieces

15g/½oz ginger, cut into julienne strips (matchsticks)

3 spring onions, cut into 3cm/1in pieces

150ml/5 fl oz Sweet & Sour Sauce (see recipe on page 149)

FOR THE GARNISH

fresh coriander leaves for sprinkling

carved red radish flower (optional)

Heat the oil in a wok until very hot. Add the pork and stir-fry for 1 minute. Add all the remaining ingredients, except for the sauce, and stir-fry for 30 seconds.

Add the Sweet & Sour sauce and bring to the boil. Cook for about 1 minute.

Transfer to a serving dish, sprinkle over the fresh coriander leaves and garnish with the carved radish flower. Serve hot.

SPARE RIBS

Kaduk Mou Yang

A Thai variation on a popular theme, these ribs are sticky, succulent but distinctly different. Marinate them for 24 hours before grilling.

makes 1 serving

1 clove garlic, peeled
2 coriander roots and stems
pinch ground white pepper
100g/3½oz sugar
½tsp salt
1½tbsp unsweetened dark soya sauce
1tbsp Blue Elephant Special Sauce
   (see recipe on page 152)

2tbsp vegetable oil
300g/10oz pork rib cage, in one piece
Green Sweet & Sour Sauce to serve
   (see recipe on page 146)

FOR THE GARNISH
green salad leaves
coriander leaves for sprinkling

In a mortar, pound the garlic with the coriander roots and stems.

Mix all the ingredients and 2tbsp hot water together except for the rib cage to make a homogenous marinade.

Immerse the rib cage and marinate for 24 hours in the refrigerator.

Grill the marinated ribs, on both sides for about 20 minutes on a low heat, preferably over charcoal, until golden-brown.

Place the ribs on a chopping board and cut between the bones to separate them, then arrange on a serving dish lined with salad leaves and sprinkle with coriander. Serve Green Sweet & Sour Sauce separately in a bowl.

THAI BEEF SALAD

Yam Nua

A spicy, lemony dressing gives a kick to this easily prepared salad. Serve it either as a component of a complete Thai meal or by itself as an original starter. (For photograph see detail on page 97.)

makes 1 serving

FOR THE DRESSING
2 bird's eye chillies
1 red chilli
2 cloves garlic, peeled
2½tbsp lemon juice
1½tbsp fish sauce
½tsp sugar

150g/5½oz grilled steak, cut into thin slices
60g/2oz cucumber, quartered lengthways, deseeded and thinly sliced

60g/2oz cherry tomatoes, halved
60g/2oz red onion, thinly sliced
1 spring onion (scallion), sliced into short lengths
1tsp fresh chopped coriander
1tsp fresh chopped Thai parsley (optional)

FOR THE GARNISH
green salad leaves
fresh coriander leaves for sprinkling
carved red radish flower (optional)

To make the dressing, pound the chillies and garlic together in a mortar, then mix with all the remaining dressing ingredients in a salad bowl.

Add the beef and remaining ingredients and toss lightly. Transfer to a serving dish lined with salad leaves, sprinkle over the coriander leaves and garnish with the carved radish flower.

CHILLIED BEEF

Nua Phad Phrik

An uncompromisingly chilli-hot dish, refreshed with al dente vegetables and a sprig of pea aubergine (eggplant). If you can't find green aubergine, increase the quantity of baby aubergine instead.

makes 1 serving

FOR THE PASTE
4 red chillies
4 cloves garlic, peeled
60g/2oz onion, sliced
1tsp Red Curry Paste (see recipe on page 151)

3tbsp vegetable oil
150g/5oz rump steak, sliced and cut into bite-size pieces, about 3mm/¹/₁₀in thick
40g/1½oz green aubergine (eggplant), quartered
30g/1oz mixed red green and yellow bell peppers, sliced

30g/1oz Spanish onion, sliced
10 baby aubergines (eggplants)
1tbsp Blue Elephant Special Sauce (see recipe on page 152)
2tbsp fish sauce
1½tsp sugar
6 Thai basil leaves

FOR THE GARNISH
fresh coriander leaves for sprinkling
carved red radish flower (optional)

Pound the paste ingredients together in a mortar or in a blender until smooth.

Heat the oil in a wok until very hot, then add the prepared paste and stir-fry for 30 seconds.

Add the beef and stir-fry for about 1 minute until it is half cooked.

Add all the vegetables, mix well then add The Blue Elephant Special Sauce, fish sauce and sugar. Stir-fry for about 2 minutes until the beef is fully cooked, then toss in the basil leaves.

Transfer to a serving dish, sprinkle with the coriander leaves and garnish with the carved radish flower.

FIRE OF SUKHOTHAI ⓥ

Yod Phaeng Phad Prik

To make the vegetarian version of this recipe, replace the beef with 80g/3oz ready deep-fried tofu cubes. The fish sauce may be replaced with light soya sauce and the chicken stock replaced with 2tbsp coconut milk. To prepare, proceed as for the recipe above.

SIDE DISHES

ROYAL FRIED RICE

Khao Phad

makes 1 serving

2tbsp vegetable oil

1 large egg

200g/7oz Plain Cooked Rice (see page 114)

30g/1oz mixed red, yellow and green bell
  peppers, finely diced

1 slice Spanish onion, finely diced

1 small piece of carrot, finely diced

30g/1oz cooked prawns

2tsp crabmeat

pinch salt

pinch ground white pepper

pinch sugar

2tsp Blue Elephant Special Sauce
  (see recipe on page 152)

1 spring onion (scallion), fairly finely sliced

FOR THE GARNISH

2 cucumber slices

1 lemon wedge

1 tomato slice

fresh coriander for sprinkling

Heat the oil in a wok until very hot. Break the egg into the oil and scramble, then add the cooked rice and mix well.

Add the bell peppers, onion, carrot, prawns and crabmeat. Stir-fry for 30 seconds.

Add the seasonings, sugar and sauce and mix well. Toss in the spring onion, mix and remove from the heat.

Transfer the fried rice to a warmed serving dish and garnish with the cucumber, lemon and tomato. Sprinkle over the coriander leaves and serve hot.

To make a vegetarian version of Royal Fried Rice, omit the prawns, crabmeat and egg, replacing them with 2tsp deep-fried cashew nuts, 1tsp raisins, 3tsp sweetcorn kernels and 2tsp snow peas. With the other seasonings, add 3tsp Sweet & Sour Sauce (see recipe on page 149).

CLOCKWISE FROM THE TOP: Sticky Rice, Royal Fried Rice and Plain Cooked Rice.

PLAIN COOKED RICE

makes 1 serving   125g/4½ oz Jasmine rice

If using loose rice, rinse it in a sieve with cold water, then drain and check for foreign bodies. If using packaged rice, follow the instructions.

Put the rice in a saucepan and add twice its volume of water, stirring briefly. Bring to the boil, cover and simmer gently for 15 minutes without further stirring. Uncover and continue to simmer for about another 5 minutes, until the rice is fully cooked and the water has evaporated. If the rice has fully absorbed the water while covered, add a little more to moisten.

STICKY RICE

Khaw Neaw

makes 1 serving   125g/4½oz glutinous rice

Rinse the rice several times in cold water until the water runs clear.

Soak for 2 hours in fresh cold water, then drain.

Line the perforated upper part of a steamer with muslin to prevent the rice falling into the water. Bring the water to the boil, put the rice in the upper part and steam for about 25 minutes, until tender and translucent.

Transfer to a serving dish and fluff up with a fork. Serve hot.

CRISPY NOODLES

Meekrob

For photograph see detail on page 111.

makes 1 serving

1 medium-sized prawn, shelled and deveined
   with tail left on
white breadcrumbs to coat
vegetable oil for deep-frying
80g/3oz rice vermicelli (noodles)
½ large egg
3½tbsp vegetable oil
15g/½oz chicken breast, minced
15g/½oz small prawns, shelled, deveined and
   chopped

1tbsp tomato ketchup
1tsp chilli sauce
6tbsp sugar
1tsp salt
2tsp lemon juice
2tsp fresh orange juice
zest 2 oranges, finely sliced

FOR THE GARNISH
fresh coriander leaves for sprinkling

Roll the medium-sized prawn in the breadcrumbs.

Heat deep-frying oil to 180°C/350°F. Dip the noodles briefly into the oil, then drain on absorbent paper and keep hot.

Beat the egg, then pour half through a fine sieve held high over the deep-frying oil. Stir it for a second or two, drain on absorbent paper and keep hot.

Deep-fry the breaded prawn for about 2 minutes, until golden-brown, drain on absorbent paper and keep hot.

Heat the 3½tbsp vegetable oil in a wok until very hot. Add the rest of the beaten egg and scramble. Add the minced chicken and chopped prawn and stir-fry for 1 minute.

Add the tomato ketchup, chilli sauce, sugar and salt while continuing to stir. Add the lemon and orange juice and zest. Lower the heat and simmer for about 3 minutes, until the mixture thickens to a syrupy consistency.

Turn off the heat and gently fold in the deep-fried noodles, making sure they are well mixed with the sauce. Remove and place on a serving dish. The noodles will become crisp as they cool. Spread the crisp fried egg over. Place the deep-fried prawn on top and sprinkle with coriander.

MIXED VEGETABLES BLUE ELEPHANT

Phad Phak

makes 1 serving

2tbsp vegetable oil
40g/1½oz baby corn, quartered
40g/1½oz Chinese cabbage, coarsely chopped
50g/1¾oz small broccoli florets
40g/1½oz mangetout
80ml/3fl oz vegetable stock

2tsp Blue Elephant Special Sauce
 (see recipe on page 152)
2tbsp oyster sauce
½tsp sugar
40g/1½oz/⅓ cup beansprouts

Heat the oil in a wok until very hot. Add all the vegetables, except for the beansprouts, and stir-fry for 30 seconds. Add the vegetable stock, sauces and sugar, then mix well. Toss in the beansprouts and transfer to a serving dish as shown in the photograph opposite.

STIR-FRIED RICE NOODLES

Phad Thai Blue Elephant

makes 1 serving

100g/3½oz rice noodles, 3mm/⅒in wide
3tbsp vegetable oil
1 large egg
10 small cooked prawns
1tbsp fish sauce
1½tbsp sugar
1tbsp lemon juice
2tsp ground dried shrimps
2tsp ground roasted peanuts
2tsp sweet turnip pickled in honey, minced or
 finely chopped

1 spring onion (scallion), cut into 2cm/¾in
 pieces
50g/1¾oz/½ cup beansprouts

FOR THE GARNISH
1 lemon wedge
carved red radish flower (optional)
1tsp ground roasted peanuts
fresh coriander leaves for sprinkling

Soak the rice noodles in cold water for 20 minutes. Heat the oil in a wok until very hot, then break the egg into the oil and scramble it. Add the prawns and noodles, then stir-fry for 15 seconds. Add the fish sauce, sugar and lemon juice. Stir-fry for a further 15 seconds, then add the dried shrimps, peanuts and sweet turnip. Continue to stir-fry for a further 15 seconds, then toss in the spring onion and the beansprouts. Mix and remove from the heat. Garnish with the lemon wedge, the radish flower with the peanuts and coriander leaves to serve.

VEGETARIAN

VEGETARIAN SPRING ROLL BLUE ELEPHANT ⓥ

Po-Pea Jay

makes 4 pieces

20g/¾oz tofu, cubed
vegetable oil for deep-frying
30g/1oz vermicelli
2 cloves garlic, peeled
2 coriander roots and stems
3tbsp vegetable oil
pinch ground white pepper
1tbsp light soya sauce
½tsp sugar
30g/1oz carrot, grated
30g/1oz white cabbage, finely sliced
½ white part of a leek, finely sliced

1 celery stick, finely sliced
1 slice onion
30g/1oz roasted peanuts, crushed
1tsp raisins
4 squares spring roll pastry, 20.5cm/8in wide
2tsp flour diluted with water into a thick paste
Red Sweet & Sour Sauce to serve
  (see recipe on page 146)

FOR THE GARNISH
green salad leaves

Deep-fry the tofu in oil heated to 180°C/350°F for about 4 minutes, until golden brown.

Soak the vermicelli in cold water for 15 minutes, then drain and cut into 5cm/2in strips. In a mortar, pound the garlic with the coriander roots and stems. Pound the tofu separately in a mortar.

Heat the vegetable oil in a wok until very hot. Add the pounded garlic, coriander and pinch of pepper, then stir-fry for 2 seconds.

Add the tofu, vermicelli, light soya sauce and sugar and stir for 30 seconds, then add all the remaining vegetables. Stir-fry for about 3 minutes, until the vegetables are cooked.

Add the crushed peanuts and the raisins. Remove the mixture from the heat and allow to cool.

To make the spring rolls, take 2tbsp of the filling and place it on a pastry square. Roll the pastry up firmly and seal with flour paste. Repeat.

Deep-fry in oil heated to 180°C/350°F for 5 minutes, then drain on absorbent paper.

VEGETARIAN VERMICELLI SALAD Ⓥ

Yam Woon Sen Jay

An intriguing and unusual combination.

makes 1 serving

100g/3½oz vermicelli
2 garlic cloves, peeled
1 large red chilli
2tbsp vegetable oil
1 celery stick, taken from the heart, with leaf, finely chopped
¼ red onion, finely chopped
2 spring onions (scallion), finely chopped
1 small carrot or ½ large one weighing 40g/1½oz, shredded
20g/¾oz cashew nuts

1½tbsp raisins
2tsp sugar (reduce amount if scaling up this recipe)
2tsp deep-fried garlic flakes
2tbsp lemon juice
2tbsp light soya sauce
2tsp roasted peanuts, crushed

FOR THE GARNISH
green salad leaves
fresh coriander leaves for sprinkling

Cover the vermicelli with cold water and soak for 15 minutes. Drain well, then cut into 5cm/2in lengths.

In a mortar, pound 1 garlic clove with the chilli.

Thinly slice the remaining garlic clove or crush in a mortar. Heat the oil and brown the garlic for a few seconds, then remove.

Plunge the vermicelli briefly into fast boiling water and drain.

Place the vermicelli in a bowl and add the ground chilli and garlic and the garlic-flavoured oil.

Add the remaining ingredients. Turn the salad gently so that it is well mixed.

Place the salad on a serving dish surrounded by green salad leaves. Sprinkle with the coriander leaves to serve.

Sweet & Sour Tofu Ⓥ

Tow-Hu Peaw Wan

makes 1 serving

80g/3oz tofu, cubed
vegetable oil for deep-frying
2tbsp vegetable oil
¼ cucumber, sliced
1 tomato, sliced
30g/1oz mixed red, yellow and green bell
   peppers, sliced
4 button mushrooms, quartered
5 pieces baby corn, quartered
1 spring onion (scallion), cut into 2cm/¾in
   lengths

1 slice Spanish onion
1 small piece root ginger, cut into julienne strips
   (matchsticks)
150ml/5fl oz Sweet & Sour Sauce
   (see recipe on page 149)

FOR THE GARNISH
fresh coriander leaves for sprinkling
carved red radish flower (optional)

Deep-fry the tofu in oil heated to 180°C/350°F for about 4 minutes, until golden-brown, then drain on absorbent paper.

Heat the vegetable oil in a wok until very hot. Add all the vegetables and ginger and stir-fry for 30 seconds.

Add the Sweet & Sour Sauce, then bring to the boil. Add the tofu and transfer to a serving dish. Sprinkle with coriander leaves and garnish with the radish flower.

DEVILLED LADIES' FINGERS Ⓥ

Chuchi Kajiab

For photograph see detail on page 119.

makes 1 serving

2 cloves garlic, peeled
2 coriander roots and stems
10 pieces small okra (ladies' fingers)
1 tsp breadcrumbs
vegetable oil for deep-frying
3 tbsp vegetable oil
2 tbsp Red Curry Paste
  (see recipe on page 151)
1½ tbsp soya sauce
2½ tbsp sugar
pinch salt

250ml/8fl oz/1 cup coconut milk
2 kaffir lime leaves, finely sliced
10 Thai basil leaves

FOR THE BATTER
80g/3oz self-raising flour

FOR THE GARNISH
1½ tbsp cream of coconut milk
fresh coriander leaves for sprinkling

In a mortar, pound the garlic with the coriander roots and stems

Make a batter with the flour and 120ml/4floz water. Coat the ladies' fingers in the batter, dip them in the breadcrumbs and deep-fry them in oil heated to 180°C/350F for about 3 minutes, until golden-brown. Drain on absorbent paper and keep hot.

Heat the vegetable oil in a wok until very hot. Add the Red Curry Paste, garlic and coriander and stir-fry for about 2 minutes until an aroma develops.

Add the soya sauce, sugar, salt and coconut milk. Bring to the boil, then add the kaffir lime and basil leaves.

Place the fried okra on a serving dish and pour the contents of the wok over them. Float the cream of coconut milk on top and sprinkle with coriander.

VEGETARIAN RED CURRY Ⓥ

Kaeng Phed

makes 1 serving

5 grapes
2 cloves garlic, peeled
2 coriander roots and stems
3tbsp vegetable oil
4tsp Red Curry Paste (see recipe on page 151)
pinch ground coriander seeds
pinch ground cumin seeds
180ml/6fl oz/¾cup coconut milk
40g/1½oz deep-fried tofu, sliced
2tsp sugar (reduce the amount if using
  pineapple canned in syrup)

1tsp salt
2tsp light soya sauce
2 kaffir lime leaves, finely sliced
40g/1½oz pineapple, preferably fresh,
  cut into small pieces
12 Thai basil leaves
1 large red chilli, sliced

FOR THE GARNISH
2tsp cream of coconut milk
fresh Thai basil for sprinkling

Remove the pips from the grapes, if any. In a mortar, pound the garlic and coriander roots and stems to a paste.

Heat the vegetable oil in a wok or saucepan until very hot. Add the Red Curry Paste, pounded garlic and coriander and the ground coriander and cumin. Stir-fry for about 3 minutes until an aroma develops.

Add the coconut milk and the tofu and bring to the boil. Add the sugar, salt, soya sauce and kaffir lime leaves and simmer for 5 minutes.

Add the grapes and pineapple and simmer for a further 1 minute. Add the basil leaves and the red chilli.

Transfer to a serving pot, float the cream of coconut milk on top of the curry and sprinkle with the Thai basil.

SWEETCORN CAKE Ⓥ

Thod Man Kao Phod

Spicy rissoles with an interesting texture.

makes 1 serving

115g/4oz self-raising flour
2tbsp Red Curry Paste
  (see recipe on page 151)
1tbsp light soya sauce
1tsp sugar
1 kaffir lime leaf, finely sliced
1 yard-long bean or 6 French beans, finely sliced
130g/4¾oz sweetcorn kernels

2tsp breadcrumbs
oil for deep-frying
Cucumber Sauce to serve
  (see recipe on page 146)

FOR THE GARNISH
green salad leaves

Put the self-raising flour in a bowl, add 6tbsp water and knead thoroughly. Add the curry paste, soya sauce and sugar, then add the kaffir lime leaf, yard-long bean and sweetcorn.

Take a quarter of the mixture and form a ball, then flatten it to form a rissole about 5mm/¼in thick and 6cm/2in in diameter. Roll in the breadcrumbs and deep-fry in oil heated to 180°C/350°F for 4 minutes. Drain on absorbent paper.

Serve hot on a serving dish on a bed of salad leaves. Serve Cucumber Sauce separately in a bowl.

VEGETARIAN COCONUT SOUFFLÉ Ⓥ

Homok Pak

makes 1 serving

FOR BLENDING
15g/½oz self-raising flour
1 coriander root and stem
1 shallot
1 thin slice fresh turmeric root
pinch ground white pepper
1 clove garlic, peeled
160ml/5½fl oz coconut milk
½tbsp Red Curry Paste
　(see recipe on page 151)
zest 1 kaffir lime
2 pieces krachai root, about 7cm/3in long
1½tbsp light soya sauce
pinch salt
½tsp sugar

1 young green coconut
60g/2oz dried tofu fairly finely sliced
4 pieces baby corn
4 button mushrooms
2tsp sweetcorn kernels

FOR THE BASE OF THE COCONUTS
1 Chinese cabbage leaf, finely sliced
10 fresh Thai basil leaves, removed from
　their stems

FOR THE GARNISH
mixed green salad leaves
2tsp cream of coconut milk
1 red chilli, sliced into very thin strips

Blend all the blending ingredients, excluding the coconut, tofu and vegetables into a homogenous mixture.

Shave off the green skin of the coconut with a sharp knife and cut the coconut in half. Empty out the water from the cavity inside the coconut.

Place the Chinese cabbage and basil leaves in the bottom of each half.

Fold the remaining ingredients into the blended mixture and divide into the coconut halves. Bring water to a heavy boil in the bottom of a steamer and steam them for 15 minutes.

Arrange the green salad leaves on a dish and place the coconut on top. Pour over the cream of coconut milk and sprinkle the strips of chilli on top.

VEGETARIAN STIR-FRIED NOODLES Ⓥ

Phad Thai Jay

A dish with a sweet and nutty note.

makes 1 serving

150g/5oz rice noodles, 3mm/⅛in wide
3tbsp vegetable oil
1tbsp light soya sauce
1tbsp sugar
2tbsp lemon juice
30g/1oz roasted and ground peanuts
1tbsp sweet turnip pickled in honey, minced or
  finely chopped
1tbsp cashew nuts, fried
2tsp raisins

1tbsp Sweet & Sour Sauce
  (see recipe on page 149)
2 spring onions (scallion), cut into sections
  about 2cm/½in long
100g/3½oz beansprouts

FOR THE GARNISH
sprinkling of roasted and ground peanuts
sprinkling of fresh coriander leaves
1 lemon wedge
carved red radish flower (optional)

Soak the rice noodles for 15 minutes in cold water, then drain.

Heat the oil in a wok until very hot. Add the noodles and stir-fry for 10 seconds.

Add the soya sauce, sugar and lemon juice, stir-fry for a further 10 seconds, then add the roasted and ground peanuts, sweet turnip, cashew nuts, raisins and Sweet & Sour Sauce. Continue to stir-fry for a further 15 seconds.

Toss in the spring onions and the beansprouts. Mix in and remove from heat.

Transfer to a serving dish and sprinkle over the roasted and ground peanuts and coriander leaves. Garnish with the lemon wedge and radish flower.

VEGETARIAN FRIED RICE BLUE ELEPHANT Ⓥ

Kaw Phad Jay

No dish of rice could be more colourful and tasty.

makes 1 serving

2 tbsp vegetable oil
280g/9½oz Plain Cooked Rice (see recipe on
　page 114)
30g/1oz mixed red, yellow and green bell
　peppers, finely diced
1 slice Spanish onion, finely diced
1 small piece carrot, finely diced
a few snow peas
pinch ground white pepper
1tbsp Sweet & Sour Sauce
　(see recipe on page 149)

pinch sugar
2tsp light soya sauce
15g/½oz cashew nuts, deep-fried
2tsp raisins
1 spring onion (scallion), fairly finely sliced

FOR THE GARNISH
2 cucumber slices
1 lemon wedge
1 tomato slice
fresh coriander leaves for sprinkling

Heat the oil in a wok until very hot. Add the rice and stir-fry for 3 minutes. Add all the vegetables except for the spring onion and stir-fry for a further 30 seconds.

Add the seasonings and sauces, nuts and raisins and mix well. Toss in the spring onion, then mix again.

Transfer to a serving dish and garnish with the cucumber, lemon wedge and tomato slices. Sprinkle over the coriander leaves and serve hot.

DESSERTS

COCONUT SORBET

makes 4 portions   2 sheets gelatine   560ml/20floz/2¼ cups can coconut milk
                     250g/9oz caster (superfine) sugar

Soak the sheets of gelatine in cold water for 15 minutes. Dissolve the sugar in half the coconut milk in a pan over heat. When the sugar is dissolved remove from the heat and allow to cool.

Add the gelatine and dissolve. Stir in the rest of the coconut milk and set aside until the mixture is completely cold. Proceed as in the recipe for Fresh Fruit Sorbets (see page 138).

COCONUT FLAN

makes 8 portions   **FOR THE CARAMEL**   350ml/12fl oz/1½ cups thick canned cream
                     160g/5½oz sugar   820ml/29fl oz/3½ cups unsweetened
                     160ml/5½fl oz water   evaporated milk
                                                              2tbsp coconut purée (or coconut cream)
                     FOR THE FLAN   4 large eggs
                     560ml/18fl oz/3½ cups coconut milk
                     3 toey leaves
                     135g/4¾oz sugar   **FOR THE DECORATION**
                                                              1½tbsp whipped cream

Dissolve the sugar in the water and boil until it reduces and turns a caramel colour. Pour into the bottom of a baking dish about 22cm/9in in diameter and 4cm/1½in deep, then set aside.

Heat the coconut milk, toey leaves and sugar in a pan, stirring to ensure the sugar is dissolved. Set aside to cool and remove the toey leaves. Add the thick canned cream, evaporated milk and coconut purée. Mix slowly in a cake mixer or by hand with a whisk. When the ingredients are well combined, add the eggs one at a time, continuing to mix. Mix for a further 3 minutes, then pour into the baking dish over the caramel.

Place the baking dish in a 'bain-marie' (a baking tray or other recipient containing water which should come halfway up the sides of the baking dish). Bake in an oven preheated to 180°C/350°F/Gas Mark 4 for 40–45 minutes.

Remove from the oven and allow to cool, then turn the flan out on to a dish caramelized side uppermost. Serve slices topped with a dollop of whipped cream.

Fresh Fruit Sorbets

A refreshing sorbet or mixture of sorbets made with fresh fruit forms the perfect cool conclusion to a spicy Thai meal.

makes 4 portions

150g/5oz caster (superfine) sugar
500g/1lb peeled, cored or stoned fruit (any kind
  of fruit can be used)
juice of 1 lemon

Make a syrup by dissolving the sugar in $3\frac{1}{2}$tbsp water as it is heated. Boil for 5 minutes, covered.

To make soft fruit sorbets, simply blend or process the fruit with the cooled syrup and the lemon juice until the mixture is smooth.

To make sorbets with hard fruit, stew it covered in the syrup until tender (up to 30 minutes according to the variety), allow to cool and add the lemon juice. Blend or process until the mixture is smooth. Place the mixture in a sorbetière and follow the maker's instructions.

If you are not using a sorbetière, place the mixture in a container, preferably aluminium (aluminum), cover tightly and put it into a freezer or freezing compartment of a refrigerator. Leave for about 40 minutes to an hour or more until the mixture is slushy and frozen around the edges. Remove and re-blend or re-process and return the mixture to the freezer. Allow to freeze for at least 30 minutes more and process again if the sorbet is not already smooth and evenly frozen. The freezing times will be longer if you use a plastic container instead of aluminium because it insulates the contents slightly.

Remove the sorbet from the freezer or freezing compartment and place in the refrigerator to soften for 20 minutes before serving.

It is possible to make sorbets from fruits canned in syrup. To a 500g can, simply add the juice of a lemon, blend or process and proceed in the same way.

Sorbets can be decorated with a little fresh fruit, prepared as for a fruit salad, or perhaps simply decorated with a sprig of mint.

COCONUT BALLS WRAPPED IN BANANA LEAVES

Sodsai

Somewhat elaborate to make, these attractive banana leaf parcels can be prepared and steamed in advance and will keep up to 3 days in a refrigerator. Reheat them for 2 minutes in a steamer or briefly in a microwave oven. (For photograph see detail on page 135.)

makes about 20 pieces

200g/7oz palm sugar
100g/3½oz grated coconut, preferably fresh
400g/14oz glutinous rice flour
1.2 litres/2 pint/5 cups coconut milk

150g/ 5oz regular rice flour
1tsp salt
1 whole banana leaf

Bring 100ml/3½fl oz water to the boil, dissolving the sugar in it. Add the grated coconut and cook for 15 minutes, stirring all the time until the mixture becomes sticky. Set aside to cool. Make about 20 little balls with the mixture, using a large heaped teaspoon for each one.

Make a dough with the glutinous rice flour and 350ml/12fl oz/1½ cups water. Cover the coconut balls with this dough and set aside on a dish or tray.

Mix together the coconut milk, rice flour and salt and simmer for 15 minutes, allowing it to thicken. Set aside.

Cut 20 oval shapes about 23cm/9in long and 16cm/6in wide and 20 rectangles about 12cm/4½in by 8cm/3in from the banana leaf. Cut 3 strips of banana leaf about 27cm/11in long and 1.5cm/½in wide.

Place the rectangles lengthways over the ovals to give two thicknesses of banana leaf in the centre, then place one of the prepared balls on top. Pour a generous 1½tbsp coconut milk sauce over the ball. Make a parcel with the banana leaves and fasten it at the top with the banana leaf strip and a toothpick. Put the parcels in a steamer for 10 minutes.

Serve the parcels warm.

Banana Cones

Kanom Kluai

makes 6 servings
(30 pieces)

330g/11½oz very ripe bananas, peeled
190ml/6½fl oz/⅘ cup coconut milk
40g/1½oz rice flour
140g/4½oz sugar

½tsp salt
80g/3oz grated coconut, preferably fresh
2 banana leaves
30 toothpicks

Mash the banana in a bowl and add the coconut milk, rice flour, sugar, salt and 60g/2oz grated coconut. Mix well.

Cut 15 circles, each 15cm/6in in diameter from the banana leaf and then cut the circles in two equal halves.

Form cones with the half circles of banana leaf, and fasten them with a toothpick, then fill them with the prepared mixture. Decorate the tops with the rest of the grated coconut.

The cones should be steamed in a vertical position in a steamer for 7 minutes (a holder can be improvised with a metal rack), then transfer to a serving dish.

JASMINE CAKE

makes 8 portions

100g/3½oz mung beans
1.75 litres/3 pint/7 cups coconut milk
500g/1lb sugar
8 large eggs
1tsp jasmine essence
10g/½oz/1tsp butter

FOR THE DECORATION
1½tbsp whipped cream
a banana leaf (optional)

Soak the mung beans for 1 hour, then boil them for about 15 minutes until cooked; drain.

Blend together the cooked beans, coconut milk, sugar and eggs.

Put the mixture in a saucepan and simmer for 15 minutes, stirring all the time. Stir in the jasmine essence.

Grease a baking dish about 22cm/9in in diameter and 4cm/1½in deep with butter, pour in the mixture and bake in an oven preheated to 180°C/350°F/Gas Mark 4 for 45 minutes.

Place slices of cake on serving plates lined with a banana leaf and decorate with whipped cream.

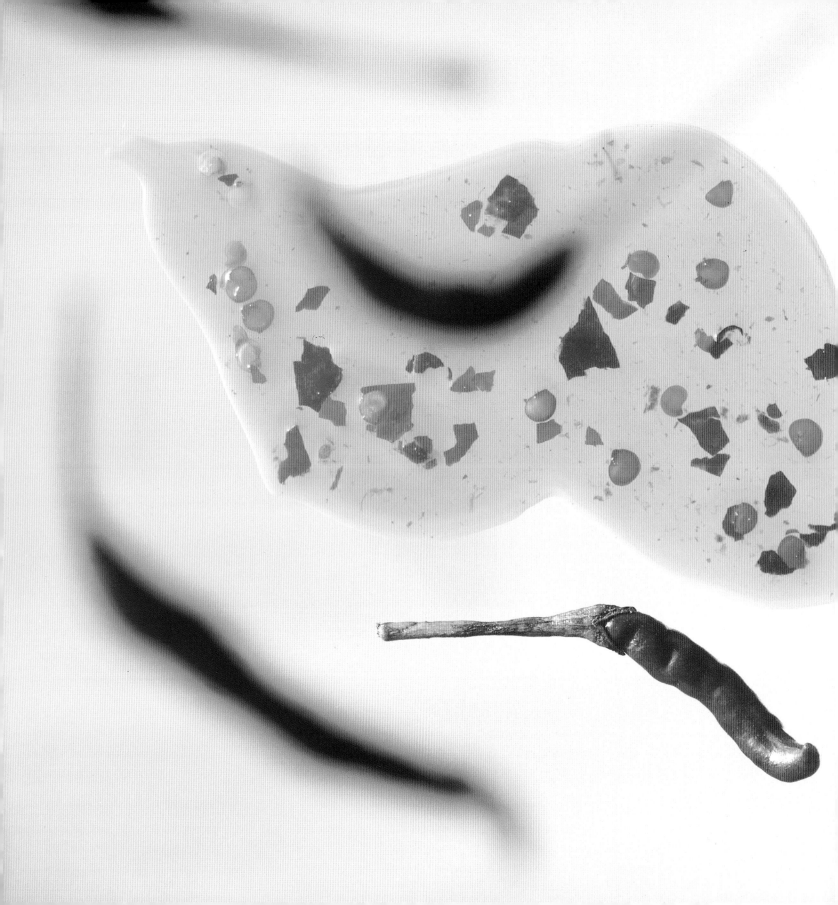

SAUCES AND
PASTES

Base for Cucumber Sauce and
Red & Green Chilli Sweet & Sour Sauce

makes 500ml/
17fl oz/2¼ cups

250g/9oz sugar
2tsp salt
2 toey leaves

1cm/½in piece of galangal
120ml/4fl oz/½ cup white malt vinegar

Bring 250ml/8½fl oz/1 cup water to the boil, add the sugar and the salt and stir well to dissolve. Add the toey leaves whole and the galangal crushed in a mortar.

Add the vinegar and simmer for 10 minutes, then strain through a sieve and allow to cool. This sauce base may be stored in the refrigerator for up to 3 months for use as required.

Cucumber Sauce

Take 7tbsp sauce base (see above) and add:

1½tbsp finely diced cucumber
2tsp finely diced shallot

1½tbsp finely diced carrot

Red or Green Chilli Sweet & Sour Sauce

Mince or grate 1 large red or green chilli and add it to 7tbsp sauce base (see above). (Wear rubber gloves if grating chillies by hand.)

Chilli Sauce (Sriracha)

Take 7tbsp sauce base (see above) and add 2tbsp chilli sauce (see page 18).

CLOCKWISE FROM THE TOP: Pineapple Sauce, Cucumber Sauce, and Tamarind Sauce.

PINEAPPLE SAUCE

makes 650ml/
23fl oz / 2¾ cups

2 red chillies, deseeded
1 yellow bell pepper, deseeded
5 cloves garlic, peeled
300g/10½oz fresh pineapple

3½tbsp white malt vinegar
1tsp salt
300g/10½oz sugar

Steam the red chillies, bell pepper and garlic for 5 minutes, then process or pound them in a mortar together with the pineapple, to form a paste.

Bring the paste to the boil, add 2tbsp water, add the remaining ingredients and simmer until syrupy. Allow to cool.

This sauce may be stored for up to 3 months in a refrigerator and used as required.

TAMARIND SAUCE

makes 375ml/
13fl oz / 1½ cups

1tsp tapioca flour
200g/7oz palm sugar
200ml/7fl oz tamarind juice

40g/1½oz sugar
3½tbsp light soya sauce

Dissolve the tapioca flour in 2tsp water, then set aside.

Bring the tamarind juice to the boil, add the palm sugar and dissolve. Add the sugar and soya sauce and stir until dissolved.

Simmer for 15 minutes, then mix in the dissolved tapioca flour. Cook for a further 1 minute, then allow to cool.

This sauce may be stored in a refrigerator for up to 3 months and used as required.

Sweet & Sour Sauce

makes 300ml/
10fl oz/1¼ cups

80g/3oz Spanish onion
5 cloves garlic, peeled
100g/3½oz pineapple
150g/5oz sugar

2tbsp vinegar
1½tsp salt
125ml/4fl oz/½ cup tomato ketchup

Liquidize the onion, garlic and pineapple into a smooth purée.

Mix in the other ingredients and bring to the boil in a saucepan, stirring gently.
Simmer for a few minutes, remove from the heat and allow to cool.

This sauce may be kept in the refrigerator for up to one week and used as required.

Dark Soya Sauce

makes 100ml/
3½fl oz/½ cup

2 cloves garlic, peeled
2tsp vegetable oil
2½tbsp dark soya sauce
2tbsp light soya sauce

1½tbsp chilli sauce
100g/3½oz sugar
3tbsp white malt vinegar

Pound the garlic into a paste. Heat the oil in a wok until very hot. Add the garlic and stir-fry for 1 second. Add the rest of the ingredients, bring to the boil and simmer for 10 minutes. Allow to cool.

PEANUT SAUCE

makes 200ml/
7fl oz/1 cup

1 clove garlic, peeled
2 coriander roots and stems
1½tbsp vegetable oil
½tbsp Red Curry Paste
   (see recipe on page 151)
160ml/5 fl oz/⅔ cup coconut milk

2tbsp ground roast peanuts
2tbsp sugar
1tbsp tamarind juice
2tsp roasted sesame seeds
1tbsp fish sauce

Pound the garlic clove and coriander roots and stems in a mortar to form a paste.

Heat the oil in a wok until very hot. Add the pounded garlic and coriander roots and the Red Curry Paste and stir-fry for 30 seconds.

Add the coconut milk, bring to the boil, then add the remaining ingredients. Cook for 5 minutes, stirring continuously to prevent the peanuts from sticking.

Remove from the heat and allow to cool.

SESAME SAUCE

makes 100ml/
3½fl oz/½ cup

10g/¼oz sesame seeds
30g/1oz red onion
40g/1½oz ginger
3tbsp white malt vinegar
2tbsp Blue Elephant Special Sauce (see recipe
   on page 152)

2tbsp light soya sauce
1tbsp dark soya sauce
¼tsp sesame oil
100g/3½oz dark brown sugar

Dry-roast the sesame seeds in a non-stick frying pan or wok for about 1 minute. Set aside.

Process or pound the red onion and the ginger, then mix into a paste with the vinegar. Bring the mixture to the boil in a pan and add all the remaining ingredients, except for the sesame seeds. Simmer for 15 minutes.

Add the sesame seeds and simmer for a further 10 minutes. Allow to cool.

RED CURRY PASTE

makes
250g / 9oz

10-15 dried red chillies, according to taste
½tsp coriander seeds
2 stems lemongrass, sliced
6 cloves garlic, peeled and sliced
60g/2oz/½ cup shallots, sliced

3tbsp galangal, sliced
1tbsp kaffir lime zest
1½tbsp shrimp paste
2tsp salt
2tsp ground white pepper

Soak the red chillies in water until soft. Dry-roast the coriander seeds in a pan for a few seconds until an aroma rises. Grind, pound in a mortar or process all the ingredients until well blended into a smooth paste, then add the salt and pepper. The paste can be kept for up to one month in an airtight container in the refrigerator or six months in a freezer.

For a vegetarian version, omit the shrimp paste.

GREEN CURRY PASTE

makes
180g / 6oz

2tsp coriander seeds
24 small fresh Thai green chilli peppers
2 stems lemongrass
3tbsp galangal, sliced
1tbsp kaffir lime zest
30g/1oz coriander root

6 cloves garlic, peeled and chopped
60g/2oz/½ cup shallots, chopped
1tbsp shrimp paste
1tsp ground cumin seeds
salt and pepper

Dry-roast the coriander seeds in a pan for a few seconds until an aroma rises. Grind, pound in a mortar or process the chillies, lemongrass, galangal, coriander seeds, kaffir lime zest and coriander root together. Mix in the remaining ingredients and grind, pound in a mortar or process until well blended into a smooth paste. Add the salt and pepper to taste. The paste can be kept for up to one month in an airtight container in a refrigerator or six months in a freezer.

For a vegetarian version, omit the shrimp paste.

YELLOW CURRY PASTE: *To make a yellow curry paste, use fresh yellow chilli peppers instead of green ones.*

For photographs see detail on page 145: from left to right, Red Curry Paste, Green Curry Paste, and Roasted Chilli Paste.

BLUE ELEPHANT SPECIAL SAUCE

While easy to make and monosodium glutamate free, Blue Elephant Special Sauce requires several hours of reduction. It may be replaced by Maggi liquid seasoning. See under Monosodium glutamate in the list of ingredients in the Going to Market *chapter (page 19).*

makes 500ml / 17fl oz / 2¼ cups

1k/2lb 4oz white cabbage, roughly chopped
500g/1lb 2oz carrot, roughly chopped
500g/1lb 2oz onions, roughly chopped
375ml/13fl oz yellow bean paste

1 tbsp salt
1 tbsp palm sugar
2½ tbsp unsweetened black soya sauce

Put the vegetables in a saucepan with 5 litres/9 pints water and the yellow bean paste. Bring to the boil and simmer over a very low heat until reduced by two thirds, stirring from time to time. This will take several hours.

Filter the liquid through a sieve and add the unsweetened black soya sauce, the sugar and the salt. Stir to dissolve.

The sauce will keep in the refrigerator for up to a week or up to three months in a freezer. To make a smaller quantity, halve all the ingredients. It is a good idea to keep the sauce in small containers or ice cube trays in the freezer so that you only need to defrost the quantity you need for a particular recipe.

ROASTED CHILLI PASTE

Nam Prik Phao

For photograph see detail on page 145. Roasted Chilli Paste is third from the right.

makes 500ml / 17fl oz / 2¼ cups

15 large dried red chillies
250ml/8fl oz/1 cup vegetable oil
30g/1oz garlic cloves, finely sliced
60g/2oz shallots, finely sliced

2tsp shrimp paste
60g/2oz palm sugar
2tbsp fish sauce
150ml/5fl oz/⅔ cup tamarind juice

Remove the seeds from the dried chillies.

Heat the oil in a wok until very hot. Add the chilli, then remove after 2 seconds. Stir-fry the garlic for about 1 minute until golden-brown, then remove. Repeat the process with the shallots.

Put the shrimp paste into the oil for a few seconds, then remove from the heat. Blend or pound in a mortar all the fried ingredients to form a paste.

Return the paste to the hot oil and fry for 2 minutes. Lower the heat, add the remaining ingredients and cook for a further 3 minutes. Remove from the heat and allow to cool.

This paste can be stored for up to one month in a refrigerator or six months in a freezer and used as required.

MASSAMAN PASTE

makes
250g / 9oz

20 dried red chillies
5tbsp vegetable oil
200g/7oz shallots, sliced
12 cloves garlic, peeled and sliced
1tsp coriander seeds
1tsp cumin seeds
1tsp white cardamom
1tsp cloves

2tsp whole black peppercorns
1tbsp galangal, chopped
1tbsp kaffir lime zest
1tbsp ground cinnamon
2tsp salt
2tsp shrimp paste
2tbsp coconut oil

Fry the chillies in the vegetable oil for a few seconds then set aside.

Fry the shallots and garlic cloves separately until golden-brown. Drain on absorbent paper and set aside.

Dry-roast the coriander, cumin, white cardamom, cloves and peppercorns in a pan then grind them together to a powder in a mortar. In the mortar, pound together or process with all the remaining ingredients, except the coconut oil, to form a smooth paste.

Cook the paste in the coconut oil for about 10 minutes until an aroma develops.

The paste can be kept for up to one month in an airtight container in the refrigerator or six months in a freezer.

THAI MENUS

Royal Symphony Menu

Serves 4

The Chillied lamb can be prepared in advance and warmed up in a pan. The chicken satays can be prepared in advance and simply grilled at the last moment. The sauce for the Bangkok fish can also be prepared in advance although the fish must be fried just before serving. If you only have one wok, use a frying pan for the fish. The cashew chicken is a typical stir-fry, to be served immediately when it is ready. Don't forget to slice the chicken and cut up the vegetables beforehand.

Songkran Menu

Serves 4

The lamb curry can be prepared in advance and warmed up. The beef salad can also be prepared in advance. It requires no cooking or heating before serving. The soup is simple to prepare, provided you have chopped, sliced and crushed the ingredients in advance. The filling for the Thai chicken soufflé can be prepared in advance and placed in the banana cups ready for steaming. The sauce and the vegetables for the Imperial fish can be cooked ahead, but should preferably not be kept hot for more than 15 minutes while the fish must be deep-fried at the last moment.

Royal Botanical Menu

Serves 4

The green curry may be prepared in advance, re-heated and garnished at the last moment. The vermicelli salad may be prepared before the remaining dishes, but not too far in advance as it may become 'tired'. The tofu soup is extremely simple and quick to cook, provided that the ingredients have already been cut, diced and trimmed. The mixed vegetables are stir-fried and should be cooked at the last moment.

Royal Siam Promenade Menu

Serves 4

If you are new to Thai cookery, we suggest that you spend a little time getting used to cooking Thai before you try this menu.

The paper prawns are quite complicated to pre-prepare, but they can be done in advance. They should be deep-fried just before serving. The Jungle salad can be prepared in advance up to the point of adding the sauce and the remaining ingredients, which should not be done until a few minutes before serving to avoid the salad being 'tired'. However, no last minute cooking is involved. The grilled duck curry can be prepared slightly ahead, but not kept hot. Re-heat and garnish at the last moment. The ginger lobster must be cooked at the last moment.

KEY PEOPLE FROM THE BLUE ELEPHANT

People . . . the heart and soul of The Blue Elephant restaurants worldwide.

NOOROR SOMANY *The secret ingredient*

Meeting Khun Nooror Somany for the first time you'd be unlikely to guess her primordial role in the creation and development of what has to be the most essential element of The Blue Elephant experience; the food on the table. Petite and still youthful in appearance, her voice is a touch childlike and she has a typically Thai aura of femininity. However, you quickly become aware first of a restless energy and, behind that, great force of character.

From a trading family with a special interest in meat and desserts – The Blue Elephant's Jasmine Cake (see page 142) is her recipe – food has always loomed large in her life. The food at home was heavily Muslim influenced and, like most Thai children, she helped her mother in the kitchen from an early age, pounding the spices for the red, green, yellow and Massaman curry pastes that are Malaysia's principal contribution to Thai cuisine. Rich Lamb (Massaman) Curry (see recipe on page 98) is traditionally served at Muslim weddings in Thailand and the same recipe Nooror learnt from her mother is used for this ever-popular dish at The Blue Elephant.

How the restaurant eventually came into being is described in *The Story of The Blue Elephant* (see page 8). Perhaps Nooror's most important contribution to its success is the adoption at the outset of Royal Thai cuisine. Travelling in the East with her husband, her observation and recall of dining out in some of the world's most distinguished restaurants were put to good use in refining customers' dining experience back in Belgium and were to stand her in good stead at the next stage in her unexpected career.

Nooror also opened The Blue Elephant in London as its original chef. But her most breathtaking exhibition of organizational ability must be the Thai food festivals she has set up in Caracas, Singapore and Tokyo.

MANUEL DA MOTTA VEIGA
A nose for fine wines

Manuel is General Manager of The Blue Elephant, Paris. A love of wine brought him into the orbit of Robert Goffard, the distinguished oenologist. Under his wing, he visited vineyards all over the world.

Since joining The Blue Elephant group in 1991, the restaurants' wine lists have been considerably enhanced and in 1995 the authoritative *Revue des Vins de France* named the Paris restaurant's wine list 'Meilleure carte de vin des restaurants exotiques de Paris' (best wine list of Paris' ethnic restaurants).

VINAI SOOKMA
Fireworks from a serene sculptor

Vinai is the son of a farmer in central Thailand. He served a long apprenticeship with a major hotel group where he was trained as a specialist in both vegetable and fruit and ice carving. He also attended the *KhaoWandee* cooking school in Bangkok and became a dessert chef, joining The Blue Elephant Group in 1996. He has carved and cooked his way around the world from Dubai to Venezuela. With The Blue Elephant he was dessert chef for two years in Paris before coming to London after a brief interlude in the Middle East.

Vinai returns to Thailand every year where nothing pleases this globetrotter more than to help his father on the family farm.

CHAROEN TIANGROJRAT
An eye for fine antiques.

Khun Charoen, whose name means lucky but who is known in The Blue Elephant group as John-John, was born and bred in Bangkok. After school he went to Seattle to study accountancy, the switched to political science.

Back in Bangkok he changed direction again, starting a business with his brother, exporting antiques to Europe. As luck would have it, one of the brothers' best customers was to be Karl Steppé, antiquarian and creator of The Blue Elephant group. When the first restaurant opened in Brussels in 1980 John-John took charge of the Bangkok export office.

This turned out to be the last twist in John-John's career path whose job has grown with the group. His expert eye is the one that selects the 120 tons of fresh vegetables, fruits, flowers an dry goods that he airfreights across the world to The Blue Elephants's kitchens every year.

CHANG *The Elephant*

His real name is Khun Rungsan Mulijan, but he is universally known as Chang, meaning elephant. A far from elephantine, youthful-looking man in his mid thirties, Chang is a partner in the group and Head Chef at the London Blue Elephant, where he has worked since it opened in 1985.

Like his colleague Madame Pa, Chang's early culinary influence was the Thai royal court, which served as a kind of finishing school for young ladies where they learned to cook and to sew. Chang's grandmother had been one such 'lady-in-waiting' and from an early age he would help her in the traditional family kitchen.

Later, Chang attended the famous Saowapha cooking school in Bangkok while working in the evenings at the mammoth Wang Keo restaurant with its three kitchens – Thai, Chinese and Japanese – and 600 covers.

He is a creative cook and returns to Thailand twice a year 'to see what's happening', travelling the country to seek out regional dishes that he then adapts for The Blue Elephant's international kitchens. A recent example is Yam Hua Pee, a banana flower salad (see recipe on page 38). He is a capable vegetable carver and his creativity spills over into devising the elaborate decorations that accompany the restaurant's regional food festivals.

Tuk *Mercurial master of salads*

For the record, Tuk's real name is Khun Galasin Krarasit. The word Tuk doesn't mean anything in particular, though it's reminiscent of *tuk-tuk*, one of those motorized rickshaws that weave their agile way like dancers through the permanent traffic jam that is Bangkok.

It's an oddly appropriate name for this small, slim and bright-eyed forty year old, who is the salad wizard of the group. It's important to remember, as recipes in this book illustrate, that Thai salads tend to be a much more substantial matter than the handful of leaves and vegetables dressed with a vinaigrette that we Westerners put together in a matter of minutes. In fact, Tuk has spent half a lifetime perfecting his craft.

He was born in a small village in the northeast of Thailand close to the Laotian border. The specialities of the region include many salads, for example, Thai Beef Salad (see recipe on page 108), with its thin slivers of freshly grilled meat. From an early age Tuk loved to cook for the family. But as soon as he was old enough, he answered the call of the big city and went to work in the kitchens of Bangkok's huge Git Pochana restaurant, seating a thousand or more diners.

Tuk remained at Git Pochana for 20 years before finally being tempted away by the group and sent to London, where he has been working since 1988. Every year, however, he returns to Thailand, not to Bangkok but to his village roots. 'It's quiet and easy-going in the village,' he says, 'not noisy like Bangkok'. Or, you might say, like Fulham Broadway, site of the London Blue Elephant. While he's there, a constant exchange of banter between him and Chang, the head chef, keeps everyone in the kitchen in stitches. When he's away an odd calm descends.

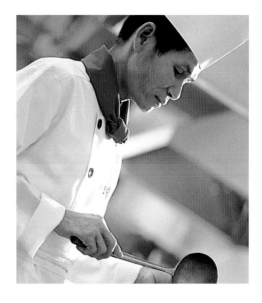

Madame Pa *Curry Queen*

Bonny, amply-proportioned Khun Sunant Wilairat is unofficial aunt to the young Thais working in the kitchens of The Blue Elephant in London. They call her Madame Pa; Pa, rather confusingly, meaning aunt.

Sunant grew up in the extended Thai royal court and learned to cook Royal Thai cuisine at her mother's knee. However, it never occurred to her that she would become a professional cook.

Later she found herself head chef of a large restaurant with nine assistants. At last there was time to show off her own twist on traditional curry recipes. Her green curry, with the addition of fresh coriander leaves (see recipe for Madame Pa's Chicken Curry on page 86), won a national prize.

In 1984 Sunant moved to the Chao Khun, a 1000-seat traditional establishment in which The Blue Elephant had an interest. This was the stepping stone to a change of continents, but Sunant Wilairat, who still speaks only Thai, was quite ready to impart her unique touch to the curries of Paris, Brussels and London. And such is her reputation that when Her Majesty The Queen of Thailand visits Europe, Sunant is summoned to prepare curries for her in the royal suites in the three capitals. Back in the kitchens of the London Blue Elephant where she is based, she remains known and loved as Madame Pa, unofficial aunt and undisputed curry queen.

Tou *Raised in the family*

Khun Souvannavong, affectionately known by the pet name of Tou, is Head Chef of The Blue Elephant in Paris. A slim-built young man with a smiling, open face he is also tall, a sure indication that he comes from the North-east of Thailand. In fact, he was born on the Laotian side of the border to a Thai mother and a Laotian father.

By the time he was thirteen years old, Laos had become a theatre of war and the family fled to Belgium as political refugees. Why Belgium?

'My dad had an uncle who'd been to Europe and he said Belgium was a peaceful place.'

Tou went to school in Brussels for a few more years, then it was time to start earning a living. Everyone knows everyone else in the small Thai community in the city, so as a teenager with no obvious career path ahead of him, he soon found himself training as a waiter at the original Blue Elephant restaurant.

'But I didn't like the job of waiter so I got myself transferred to the kitchen where I started out as a "plongeur" – doing the washing up.'

It was in the kitchen that the tide began to turn for the plongeur. He was fished from the soapy waters of the sink by Laaiet and Teo, the very first Blue Elephant cooks and major contributors to setting the standards that became the group's hallmark.

Tou's growing skills and versatility coincided with the expansion of the group and he found himself standing in for the absent chefs in London, Paris and Copenhagen. Then, in 1992, he settled in Paris as an under-chef. He was promoted to Head Chef in 1997.

Sathit Srijettanont *High Thai flyer*

Still in his mid-twenties, Khun Sathit Srijettanont, known more simply as Joe, is a representative of the new generation of Blue Elephant people. Head Chef of the Brussels restaurant, his manner combines professional assurance with a quiet sense of humour.

Joe was born in Thailand and at twelve years old was already learning to cook from his father, who passed on many of those secrets that can only be acquired by practice. More formal training followed with six years of food and beverage studies at high school from which he graduated with the best student award.

While never losing sight of his Thai roots and with his early grounding in Thai cuisine, Joe's career was firmly set on an international course by a further two years of hotel management study at Wemmel in Belgium followed by the conventional budding chef's tour of France, working in a number of restaurant kitchens.

After a brief interlude with Thai Airways International, Joe made a final landing at the Brussels Blue Elephant. His professional skills soon led naturally to his being put in charge of large scale banqueting. In this role he was able to develop and use his special interest in the latest catering technology. At the same time he benefited from the expertise in the traditions of Royal Thai Cuisine of the group's most experienced chefs.

Joe became Head Chef at the Brussels Blue Elephant in 1997. He was also responsible for preparing and styling the food for the photographs in this book.

INDEX